First English edition published by Colour Library Books Ltd.
©1987 Illustrations and text: Colour Library Books Ltd.,
   Guildford, Surrey, England.
This edition published by Arlington House.
hgfedcba
Display and text filmsetting by Acesetters Ltd.,
   Richmond, Surrey, England.
Color separations by Llovet S.A., Barcelona, Spain.
Printed and bound in Barcelona. Spain by Cronion, S.A.
ISBN 0 517 554879
All rights reserved.
ARLINGTON HOUSE 1987
Dep. Leg. B-36493-87

SEXUAL POSITIONS

A PHOTOGRAPHIC GUIDE TO PLEASURE AND LOVE

Text by

Glenn Wilson, Ph.D.

Photography by Peter Barry

ARLINGTON HOUSE

PREPARATIONS FOR SEX

In the film *Last Tango in Paris*, Marlon Brando and Maria Schneider meet by chance while inspecting a vacant flat that each is interested in. By way of introduction, and before uttering a word, they perform standing intercourse on the stairway, fully clothed. Thus is the flat-sharing contract arrived at.

This is all very well in exceptional (usually fictional) circumstances, but most people take a little longer to get aroused! Some degree of preamble or foreplay is usually called for. And just as a spontaneous quickie can be particularly exciting, so may a deliberately long and teasing session of foreplay expand our enjoyment of a sexual encounter. Sex is, or at least should be, much more than the proverbial "wham, bam, thank you ma'am".

Creating the mood

Foreplay is often necessary because a woman's sexual response cycle moves through its sequence at a slower rate than that of the man. A man may be aroused at the mere sight of an attractive, well-endowed young woman, especially if she is in the process of removing her clothes provocatively. For most women, however, some sort of longer term, contextual build-up is required before they are ready for sex. This may begin with romantic and chivalrous gestures of affection such as presenting flowers, opening a car door or providing a supportive elbow. It may continue with soft, loving words intoned in a deep, reassuring voice and the assumption of competent physical control of the situation - anything from leading a dance to picking her up and carrying her "across the threshold" into the bedroom. Despite the odd feminist protestation to the contrary, most women do long for a "knight in shining armour on a white charger" who will sweep them off their feet and "possess" them in a firm but caring way.

Once in the bedroom, the build-up may be continued with gentle caresses and kisses to parts of the body that are not too directly stimulating. Going "straight to the button" may be reacted to as a form of annoyance, but if the lips are pressed slowly and warmly to the inside of the wrist, the back of the neck, or the ear lobes, a woman is much more likely to 'melt'. If a woman is uncertain as to whether she is feeling sexy it is more fruitful to offer her massage than intercourse; she is more likely to accept and quite likely to be brought to a state of readiness as a result of the pleasure and relaxation that the massage gives her. Sex therapists experienced in the treatment of female unresponsiveness stress the importance of loving, non-threatening, bodily caresses without pressure towards, or obligation to, intercourse as a means of inducing sexual receptiveness ("sensate focusing" is their jargon for this exercise).

In recent years it has become fashionable to argue that female reserve with respect to sex is a superficial product of a Victorian upbringing that is selectively imposed on girls rather than boys. In this view, increasing equality and permissiveness in society will finally release women from their traditional inhibitions, making them just as readily arousable and pleasure-seeking as men. Unfortunately (or perhaps rather fortunately) there is a limit to the extent to which changes in

social mores will unleash female sexuality which is set by the particular biological nature of women. Because throughout evolutionary history it was the female who stood to get pregnant as a result of sexual intercourse, she progressively acquired a degree of caution in sexual matters in order that her

precious eggs and nurturant skills were not squandered on the offspring of the wrong male at the wrong time. Universal nymphomania may be an appealing fantasy to some playboy males, but it is most unlikely to eventuate, whatever the role-prescriptions that society devises.

Expansion of awareness

Although it is most usually women who appreciate protracted foreplay, men can also be beneficiaries. Men who are inclined to be impotent because of anxiety, age, exhaustion, previous bad experiences, boredom with a particular partner, or a generally low libido, may equally need some time to warm up. Not all men can produce an immediate erection on demand like clockwork; animals they may be, but not robots. Some men need as much time to savour love-making as any woman. The differences between the sexes apply only on average; there is a great deal of variation within sex and a great deal of overlap between the sexes.

Even if a man is instantly and reliably aroused, he may be brought to a state of enhanced performance and ecstasy by the kind of teasing that is often involved in foreplay. One application of this principle is the "start-stop" or "squeeze" technique that sex therapists use for the treatment of premature ejaculation. The man is repeatedly brought close to the point of climax by manual or oral stimulation and then prevented from coming with a squeeze of the fingers towards the end of his penis. If he is also given a little time for excitement to subside on each occasion when the squeeze is applied, his performance may be drawn out for a long period of time and the eventual release becomes all the more intense.

Many of the so-called "sadomasochistic" activities such as

spanking, bondage and humiliation can be thought of as yoga-like ordeals which lead to an expansion of consciousness. Their key elements of restriction, deprivation, control, and mild fear-induction are seen in religious and magical rites of many kinds. Orgasms can be all the more exciting if they are developed over a long period of time; if an element of tension or "threat" is introduced, and if permission for release is withheld to the point of near distraction.

This is one of the reasons why so many psychiatrically unimpeachable couples play bedroom games like slave and master, teacher and pupil, doctor and patient, rapist and victim, prostitute and client. Apart from enjoyment derived from the mental tingle of "naughtiness" the controlling party can extract performances and induce experiences that the "submissive" party did not know existed in his or her repertoire. To classify such behaviours as perverted or to describe them in the language of psychopathology is to demean a highly creative and exploratory aspect of the human spirit.

The female orgasm

In developing the art of foreplay it is useful to understand the elusive nature of women's orgasm. When a woman does have an orgasm it seems to be very much the same as that experienced by a man. Of course, ejaculation does not occur, but the muscles of the vaginal wall show the same rhythmic contractions as those of the urethra (timed at 0.8 second intervals). Descriptions of the sensation of orgasm provided by men and women are fairly indistinguishable, with the exception that some women, but no men, report multiple orgasms.

The real difference between men's and women's orgasms is in the speed, ease and reliability with which they occur. A small proportion of women (perhaps 10%) claim they always achieve orgasm during sex, a similar proportion never have orgasm, but most have them intermittently and have to work at them to some extent. What is more, the majority of women can obtain orgasm more reliably with a vibrator or by their own fair hand than during intercourse with a male partner.

To explain this state of affairs it is necessary to consider the difference in biological nature between men and women. In men, orgasm has a clear function - it is the experience accompanying ejaculation which is both intensely rewarding and followed by satisfaction, and which allows termination of intercourse. An identical mechanism in women would be counter productive because it would interfere with the female strategy of reserve and selectivity in matters of sex, and would result in intercourse being terminated 50% of the time before ejaculation had occurred. In fact, the current thinking among evolutionary theorists is that the female orgasm has no biological function at all, but is simply a spin-off of the fact that females share with the male necessary neurological equipment. The clitoris is a vestigial penis that is perhaps more functional than the nipples of a man, but is in many respects comparable. It is useful as a focus for excitement, which leads to psychological receptiveness and vaginal lubrication, but orgasm is not essential to conception or even to the enjoyment of sex for many women. Likewise, some men enjoy sucking of their nipples even though this has no biological

usefulness, yet nobody has seriously maintained that men who do not gain erotic enjoyment from their nipples should be referred for sex therapy.

Of course, women do experience frustration if they are brought close to the point of orgasm by a long period of stimulation and then suddenly left high and dry. Also, there is little doubt that they gain immense pleasure from orgasm once they have learned to achieve it. Therefore it is useful to understand that the occurrence of female orgasm usually depends on a long period of clitoral stimulation. The movement of the penis inside the vagina may cause the clitoral hood to stretch and slide backwards and forwards across the clitoris itself, as Masters and Johnson observed, but this is not sufficient stimulation to bring all women to orgasm. Some sort of more direct contact may be required, whether manual, oral, mechanical, or through the female-superior position for intercourse that is so often recommended by sex therapists.

It appears that the female genitalia are not ideally designed for orgasm during intercourse. The clitoris may be well-positioned for the early stages of arousal, which promotes lubrication, but it misses out on the major action later on. Testimony to this is the fact that women seldom masturbate by inserting phallic shaped objects inside their vagina; more commonly they manipulate the area of the clitoris, or place a flat-headed vibrator against it. Asked about "sex in the best of all possible worlds", one of Shere Hite's subjects replied: "My clitoris would be in my vagina, for Christ's sake, so I could come when I fuck". As it is, most women require some additional outside stimulation either before, during, or after sexual intercourse if orgasm is to be achieved. The considerate man does not simply roll over and go to sleep as soon as he is satisfied, but makes some enquiry about the condition of his female partner. She, in turn, should not wait passively for orgasm to be "given to her" by what her man is doing; it helps enormously if she takes an active part, thrusting her pelvis up and down and ensuring that stimulation is directed towards the most gratifying areas.

The Grafenberg Spot

Although women do not usually ejaculate in the same way men do, some women are reputed to produce an emission that is neither urine nor lubrication but something similar to male semen without the presence of sperm. In a small minority of women, this emission appears as a sudden spurt at the moment of orgasm and may cause them to think they have wet the bed. The carrying fluid of male ejaculate is produced by the prostate gland in men, so attention has focused on the possible role of prostate analogues in women. Some North American researchers claim recently to have rediscovered an extremely sensual zone that was initially identified, some decades ago, by the German gynaecologist, Dr Grafenberg. This is a small area set about an inch underneath the anterios (upper) wall of the vagina, behind the public bone and about halfway along towards the cervix. This is supposedly a particularly sensitive area of the female internal anatomy and the one that may trigger the fabled emissions in a minority of woman (which come from the urethra, incidentally, not the vagina). It may be further speculated that such women have unusually well-developed prostate equivalents and are man-like in this respect, just as some women have unusually large clitorises that appear as tiny penises.

Since there seem to be considerable individual differences among women with respect to the location and sensitivity of erogenous zones a certain amount of mutual exploration, both physical and verbal, may pay great dividends. A woman may investigate the sensitivity of her own Grafenberg zone by inserting her forefinger inside the vagina about two inches and manipulating the upper wall quite rhythmically and deeply. Initially, an urge to urinate may be felt, but in some women this gives way to mounting sexual excitement. Some sex therapists believe the G-spot is just as useful a key to orgasm as the clitoris; excessive stimulation of the clitoris becomes painful to some women, whereas massage of the G-spot may remain pleasurable for much longer. In a man the equivalent area to the Grafenberg spot is the region between the anus and the underside of the testicles, since this is closest to the prostate. Pressure here, or indeed inside the rectum on the upper wall, may similarly provoke excitement and orgasm. Some men like their anus manipulated with a finger or object such as a candle during intercourse.

Kissing and Hugging

Kissing is a practice that appears in a variety of forms around the world and has varying significance, sexual and social. In Western society, it normally takes the form of a couple pressing their lips together; in some Pacific cultures, however, intimacy and affection is communicated by rubbing noses. A kiss may be used to signify affection on greeting or departure, and there is no need for sexual arousal to be involved, especially among family members or old friends. At the other extreme is the long episode of deep, passionate kissing sometimes called "necking" and which may include "French kissing" - exploration of the inside of each other's mouth with the tongue. This may be very arousing and used as a prelude to sexual intercourse, although not necessarily; some teenagers treat it as an end in itself. In the same way hugging may simply be affectionate and reassuring or it may be the commencement of an erotic episode.

Some ethologists believe that kissing derives from the mouth-to-mouth feeding of a child by its mother that is common in birds but also seen in some primitive human cultures. More important is the opportunity to identify a loved one by smell; the close facial intimacy that occurs in kissing permits parent-child imprinting based on smell and facilitates a similar form of pair-bonding between lovers. The smell of cigarette smoke or garlic on the breath of a potential lover may be disastrous to a developing relationship if the other party does not share the habit.

There is also a testing function involved in courtship kissing. If a girl turns her cheek to a proffered kiss following a first date, rather than receiving it fully on the lips, she can communicate a degree of coolness to her suitor. If she reciprocates with great passion and abandon, throwing her body squarely around him, a rather different message will be conveyed. Thus kissing is a social signalling arena that is in some ways less threatening and embarrassing than explicit verbal negotiation. Nobody has to throw all their cards on the table at once. Approach and withdrawal can be undertaken and suggested without great loss of face on either side.

As most love manuals instruct, kissing need not be restricted to the mouth-to-mouth form. Application of the lips to many other areas of the body can be extremely erotic, and most people like to be kissed slowly all over. Areas that might be singled out for special attention include the neck, shoulders, ear-lobes, forearms, breasts, buttocks, inside thighs and the soles of the feet, as well as the lips and genitals. Alex Comfort recommends a procedure called "making a carpet of flowers", which involves covering the whole body from head to toe with small, close kisses.

Oral Sex

Oral sex comes in two main forms - kissing, licking and sucking the vulva (cunnilingus) and equivalent mouth contact with the penis (fellatio). The term cunnilingus derives fron the Latin word *cunnus*, meaning the female part, and *lingere* (licking). Fellatio comes from *fellare*, which means to suck. The simultaneous performance of these two activities upon each other by two people is known as *soixante-neuf* (or as the French call it, sixty-nine). This is because the shape of the number (69) is reminiscent of the orientation of the couple so occupied.

Oral sex may be used as a complete sexual experience in itself, with both partners being brought to orgasm in this position. More often, though, it is a part of foreplay - a preamble to genital intercourse. As such it has certain advantages; lubrication is much more readily provided by the mouth than by the vagina, and this can be used to initiate excitement. Saliva is, in fact, a good rival to commercial sex lubricants such a KY Jelly. Also, the mouth has more self-control than one's own genitalia and can therefore be used to "tease" the partner much more effectively. The trouble with immediate genital contact is that it may all be over too quickly; oral excitement can be drawn out for a much longer time if the partners are skilled at recognising the approach of each other's climax.

For many women cunnilingus is more exciting than intercourse because the tongue is self-lubricating, reliably firm, darts around with great agility and can play directly about the area of the clitoris, from whence excitement and orgasms are triggered. Similarly, for a man,, fellatio is particularly exciting because it is different (like a new vagina); because it signifies a high degree of intimacy, and because the woman plays the active, assertive role (like a holiday to some men who are used to doing all the work). It is particularly effective as a way of restarting a man for a second round of lovemaking ("reviving the dead" as it has been called).

If the man should ejaculate in the woman's mouth there is no danger in swallowing his semen, it is good healthy protein, though possibly a bit salty and not to every woman's taste. There is no point in remonstrating: it is said that the three most useless promises, in reverse order, are: "the car is on its way", "the cheque is in the post", and "don't worry, I won't come in your mouth".

According to sex therapist Avodah Ovitt, fellatio has a rich history, however apocryphal. Lipstick is supposed to have originated from classical prostitutes who wore it to signify their willingness to perform oral sex. Cleopatra was reported to be a supreme fellatrix; the claim is made that she "lowered herself" on 106 Roman legionnaires in one night. Some historians maintain that it was a custom amongst grandmothers, mothers and nursemaids in ancient China to calm little boys by fellatio, and anthropologists have described Melanesian cultures in which young boys are required to fellate older boys in order to share magically in their strength and virility, as well as to provide them with a sexual outlet prior to marriage.

Prior to Kinsey, people were very reticent about discussing the practice of oral sex since it was regarded as an unusual perversion. The Kinsey reports revealed, however, that oral sex was quite widespread even in the 1940s, with around half of all Americans indulging, especially the better educated. Since that time, and probably partly as a result of Kinsey's "normalisation" of the practice, oral sex has become even

more popular, with the vast majority of people trying it at least occasionally. A recent survey of sexual practices in Britain found that 90% of both men and women had tried oral sex and nearly all of them had enjoyed it immensely.

There are certain dangers to oral sex that should be mentioned. (1) Although the risks to health are not really any greater than intercourse itself, or even deep kissing, some of the common forms of V.D. can be communicated in this way if they are present. The so-called "sexually transmitted diseases" would probably be better called "diseases of mucosal apposition", since they attack mucous membranes, whether in the mouth, the vagina or the urethra. Washing is a basic courtesy before having oral sex for aesthetic reasons but it does not provide much protection against V.D. Syphilis and gonorrhoea are much less fearsome in the modern age of antibiotics; the current worry is herpes, which is less intrusive but apparently incurable.

(2) Cunnilingus is not recommended in connection with spermicidal contraceptives; they are not usually very poisonous but may be rather unpleasant tasting. There is no danger in cunnilingus during the woman's period, though just about everyone except Count Dracula finds it more pleasurable towards the middle of the cycle.

(3) The term 'blow-job' is misleading to the novice, since blowing into the genitals is not the way oral sex should be performed. Not only is it unpleasurable, but it can be positively dangerous. For example, vigorous blowing into the vagina of a pregnant woman can force air bubbles into the blood vessels, which in the extreme could be fatal to mother and foetus.

(4) Fellatio can result in a lacerated penis unless the woman is careful with her teeth and the man reasonably controlled in his thrusting movements. On very rare occasions it has been known to cause death by asphyxiation by plugging up the larynx. With a minimal degree of care and consideration on each side neither laceration or gagging should be a problem.

(5) Finally, it should be mentioned that in the outmoded laws of some countries, including many American States, oral sex, even between married couples, is illegal and punishable by jail. Although seldom enforced, this provides the opportunity for blackmail and vindictive revenge by an angry partner or spouse. This, then, may be another reason why oral sex should only be conducted with a partner who is truly loved and trusted.

Bedroom manners

There is a prime rule of etiquette for lovers which is that love-making should be set apart from the mundane and difficult aspects of the relationship. Domestic and other disputes should be left outside the bedroom door and the atmosphere inside kept positive, warm and supportive. This may seem contrived at times, but it is important that the playful quality of sex is not disturbed by unrelated areas of conflict and unhappiness.

By the same token, the things that are done and the fantasies aired during love-making should be kept within that 'watertight' compartment and not carried back into real life. Your lover's little idiosyncracies and preferences should not be used against them in public or private to belittle, deride or embarrass. They should remain an unspoken secret shared between the two of you. It is extremely bad form, for example, to use the relaxation and trust of love-making to extract confessions of fact or fantasy only to remonstrate and recriminate the following morning. If there is to be any confessional in the bedroom, expiation (punishment, forgiveness, etc.) should be worked out on the spot. Likewise, it is usually counterproductive to discuss your partner's sexual performance (especially its deficiencies) over breakfast or in the cold light of day. This also should be dealt with at the time in a sympathetic, good-humoured and constructive way, rather than in the mode of complaint or condemnation. Only by keeping your sex-life separate from the other areas of conflict

which inevitably arise in the course of an extended relationship can sex remain fresh and fun-filled for a long time.

POSITIONS FOR SEX

Contrary to fable, there are only two major positions for coitus. One is frontal, or face-to-face, and the other is rear entry, or face to back. Either of these may, however, be performed in various orientations - lying down, sitting, standing, swinging from the chandelier, and so on - and this provides an almost infinite variety of sexual acrobatics.

Missionary position

This is one way of describing the most standard frontal position of the man lying on top of the woman and between her legs. It is often thought that it acquired its title because the Victorian European missionaries in Africa and Oceana had difficulty in converting the natives to this method when they favoured more primitive, "brutish" copulation attitudes. In fact, the "missionary position" is standard in virtually all known cultures, so if the label has any valid meaning at all, it must refer to attempts made by some Christian missionaries to stamp out all alternatives that they considered bestial or perverted.

Missionary position is probably popular because it allows the man to be dominant (which seems to be a natural instinct) while at the same time permitting facial communication (which may be considered human, polite, or an additional turn-on). The main disadvantage is that the weight of the man may not allow the woman sufficient freedom of movement for her to obtain satisfaction. A common variant, therefore, is for the man to take some or all of his weight on his elbows or hands, thus lifting himself clear of his partner and allowing her more opportunity to move and breathe.

Hairpin

If, starting from missionary position, the woman lifts her legs and folds back as far as she can towards her ears, we reach a position (or contortion?) which might be called "hairpin". The man may assist by taking hold of her legs somewhere towards the ankles and (gently) holding them back.

This position provides very deep penetration (sometimes too deep, depending on the size of the organs). Partly for this reason, it is recommended to couples who want to achieve pregnancy. If this is the aim, the woman is best to stay *in situ* for a little while after ejaculation, so the sperm have every chance to permeate the upper reaches of the vaginal canal.

Flanquette

Another variation on the basic missionary position is for the man to pass one of his legs outside a leg of his partner, so that male and female legs are in effect alternated. This usually means that the man's weight is transferred somewhat onto one of his elbows, and the couple are halfway towards a side-by-side position. The title of this variation refers to the fact that the inner thighs are involved in erotic contact.

Flanquette may be a very satisfying elaboration to both parties, since it retains some elements of male dominance, while at the same time not smothering the woman, and often increasing the degree of labial and clitoral stimulation. Most couples find that in using flanquette, they "dress" consistently either to the left or the right, according to what seems natural and comfortable to them.

Oriental style

Various forms of squatting and sitting up together tend to be associated with the Japanese and Chinese, partly, perhaps, because of the image conveyed by their early (especially eighteenth century) erotic prints. Such positions are usually practiced on cushions on the floor, partly because of Oriental tradition and partlybecause it is hard to maintain balance on springy, Western beds.

These positions allow for a great deal of intimate facial communication, as well as yoga-style control, which can prolong the activity considerably. In this matter, the two partners are equal, as either can initiate or restrict movement.

If both partners then lean backwards, a position is reached that is sometimes called "X-position". If hands are held and arms fully extended, a kind of see-saw motion can be enjoyed. The backward pull on the man's penis may delay his orgasm and permit prolonged intercourse that is very stimulating to the woman.

Roman ride

This refers to the increasingly popular "female superior" or woman-on-top position. This was little used by married couples in Victorian times because it was considered indelicate for women to be lusty and active in the bedroom. It is, however, well documented in classical Roman and Indian literature, so cannot be claimed as a modern feminist discovery.

Sex therapists recommend it to women who have orgasm difficulty since it gives them a great deal of freedom and control as well as opportunity for clitoral stimulation. From this vantage, the woman can dictate timing, angles, and depth of penetration, and can usually learn how to gain her climax before that of her partner. The ride may be performed facing backwards as well as forwards; this provides new visual stimulation for the man, but penetration may be too deep for comfort in some couples.

Few men are so insecure in their masculinity that they are threatened by adopting the submissive role every so often. Most enjoy it immensely, especially if the woman has good vaginal muscle control and can draw on him like a vacuum cleaner. The weight of the woman is not usually as troublesome as the weight of the man on her can be.

While highly recommended for mutual pleasure, Roman ride is not the best way of achieving pregnancy. The semen tends to lose concentration by running out of the vagina. However, pregnancy is still very possible, so it should not be thought of as a contraceptive device.

Sometimes the penis will fall out of the vagina if the woman lifts herself too high, resulting in what has been described as "the fastest four-handed game in the world". Worse still, she may hurt the man by crashing down on his semi-erect penis after it has slipped out of the haven. For this reason it is usually best to sustain a fairly easy canter rather than trying to win the rodeo.

Doggy fashion

This is a slander on the standard rear entry position, which is every bit as natural and pleasurable as frontal intercourse. In awkward terrain such as mountain-tops, river beds and aeroplane toilets it is also a great deal more comfortable and practicable for the woman simply to bend over, with the man standing behind her. When lying together in bed, rear entry is one of the gentlest and snuggest approaches - it may even be done while half asleep.

Facial communication is, of course, restricted in this position, but then not everyone's face is an optimum erotic stimulus, and it is sometimes a relief not to have to worry about conversation during sex. Some businessmen boast a preference for dictating into a machine while their secretary performs a more indispensable service bent over the desk! Fantasies may also be more freely engaged when social demands are reduced.

Some critics of the method point out that the woman's clitoris is left out of the action to a large extent, so she might have difficulty in coming. This can be easily corrected by digital attention to the area by the man, who can quite easily reach around her belly. His hands are also free to caress her bottom, breasts, and inside thighs, all of which can add to excitement.

Rear entry should not be confused with anal intercourse, or sodomy, as some of the puritan objectors seem to do. That is a whole different ball game, and much less satisfactory to most couples as well as being illegal in Britain and many other countries. The direction usually given to young men is "second down from the back of the neck"!

Wheelbarrow

A celebrated adaption of rear entry, that may seem more like a circus trick than a sensible love-making variation, is called "wheelbarrow". As the name implies, the man lifts the woman's legs from the floor while she rests on her elbows or walks on her hands. Since this places her head low in relation to her body there is a run of blood to the head which adds to the sensation of orgasm. Not all women find this pleasurable, but it is safer than the throttling games some sensation-hungry people have been known to play.

Knee trembler

As practised in shop doorways by many an urban youth, and up against trees in the country, this is the stand-up quickie that requires a minimum of undressing. Both parties need to be fairly excited to begin with because penetration is otherwise difficult. Sometimes it helps if the woman lifts one leg and wraps it around her partner's waist - a position that Eastern manuals call "climbing the tree". Or, if she is reasonably light and lithe, she may bring up the other leg as well and grip him around the bottom. The obviates any difficulties of height discrepancy, although another solution to this problem is to perform on the stairs. None of the stand-up positions have much of a reputation for promoting female orgasm, although some of them may be used to prolong intercourse.

EXOTIC SETTINGS

If your love-life is flagging you might think it is time to change your partner. Indeed you may be right – but this can be extremely inconvenient socially and there is one thing you definitely ought to try first – and that is changing the background. Many couples who have made love year after year in the same bed, with the same wallpaper and curtains, find their sex lives are mysteriously revitalized when they go on holiday and stay with somebody else or in an hotel. Although they may put this down to rest or "the change of air", the visual novelty of the surroundings is probably more instrumental in this revival of libido. Clearly, boredom is a function of places as well as of people.

Beyond the bedroom

What are the possibilities? You can redocarate your bedroom, giving particular thought to creating an erotic atmosphere, for example by introducing a large water-bed, or a four-poster with canopy, dimmer switches on the lights, candelabras, silk sheets, purple drapes, deep-pile carpet, erotic art, strategically placed mirrors, a sound-system or video playback for special movies. Hugh Heffner (creator of the Playboy Empire) favours a circular bed so that he can "do the round"; making love at all points of the compass. For ideas, you may visit one of the X-rated motels that abound in California (a kind of Disneyland for adults). Although these establishments specialize in the extra-marital trade, some married couples spend an occasional night in one for inspiration.

Should all this seem to you contrived and artificial, you can try other rooms in the house that you do not usually think of as venues for sex, such as the lounge or bathroom. The light from the TV set in the lounge can be quite romantic, and if you choose the right kind of erotic programme this can also enhance your love-making. The advantage of the bathroom is that you are usually nude and clean, both of which have obvious benefits, and there are usually mirrors about for voyeuristic titillation.

If making love under the house or in the attic be careful of spiders, loose tacks and perished electrical wiring. Otherwise you may get a kick that is beyond your optimum - sufficient perhaps to propel you through the roof and into your neighbour's vegetable patch, where you are bound to look very silly.

Love alfresco

This brings us to the topic of outdoor sex. There is something very exciting about going back to nature, making love among trees, flowers, long grass and mountains, under the yellow sun or the silver moonlight, and with the sound of rivers, waterfalls or breakers on the beach rushing in our ears. One need only think of the classic honeymoon venues such as Niagara Falls, Hawaii, Bermuda and Switzerland to appreciate the significance of natural scenery and the inspiration that may be provided by the elements.

One can invoke obscure scientific explanations for our enhanced virility in these situations. Sunlight, for example, has the capacity to activate sex hormones and thus raise libido; moonlight is purported to bring out the "wolf" in us and promote a zany, lustful frame of mind. Rushing water increases the concentration of negative ions in the atmosphere which is said to improve our general state of health and induce feelings of well-being. The sound of a beach or waterfall approximates to "white noise" (a random distribution of frequencies) which is known to have analgesic and relaxant properties. Trees consume carbon dioxide and emit oxygen in return, thus improving the quality of the air. But all of these physiological processes are probably secondary to the direct psychological lift we experience when immersed in aesthetically beautiful surroundings.

Again there are certain hazards to be wary of: insect bites, stinging nettles, poison ivy, avalanches, and trigger-happy deer hunters, who sometimes shoot at anything that moves and only afterwards try to identify it. Sand in the works can also be very uncomfortable. In Australasia sex in the sandhills is affectionately known as "concrete mixing" - a distressing image which, of course, does little to deter the teenage enthusiast. One adventurous New Zealand friend claims to have consummated his marriage at twelve and a half thousand feet on the top of Mt Cook, which is fine if you're not afraid of frostbite!

Another possible hazard of outdoor sex is discovery by penal authorities. Recently, two British tourists were sentenced to jail for getting carried away and making love publicly on a Greek beach. Apparently, a crowd of several hundred spectators had assembled to watch the performance before the police arrived to spoil everybody's fun. No private citizen had seen fit to intervene, as they might have done if the pair had been fighting, yet the court was totally unsympathetic to the hapless young lovers. Similarly, in Britain, when a well-known businessman was discovered having oral sex with a girl-friend on the band-stand in a public park, the court proceedings destroyed his marriage. In this case, the couple were charged with indecency even though it was pitch dark, the park was closed for the night, and the act was witnesses only by the constable who shone his torch on them. In a rather more liberated precedent, the Italian courts have just ruled that sexual intercourse in a car is legal if the couple are sufficiently passionate to steam up the windows.

Isolation and risk

Ship-board and holiday romances are well recognized occurrences. The magic of a new environment seems to have power to stimulate sexual exploits that would never be contemplated at home. With respect to long-distance cruises it is fabled that young women "leave their virginity at the gang-plank". And indeed, there is something uniquely liberating about being isolated within a circumscribed social group away from one's family, previous contacts, and the community at large. The rest of the world effectively ceases to exist and the old prohibitions no longer apply. Powerful rapport is quickly established with other people who are "all in the same boat" figuratively or literally, and sexual interest is catalysed by the suntans, colourful clothes and freedom from care and responsibility, as well as the excitement engendered by the novelty of the surroundings.

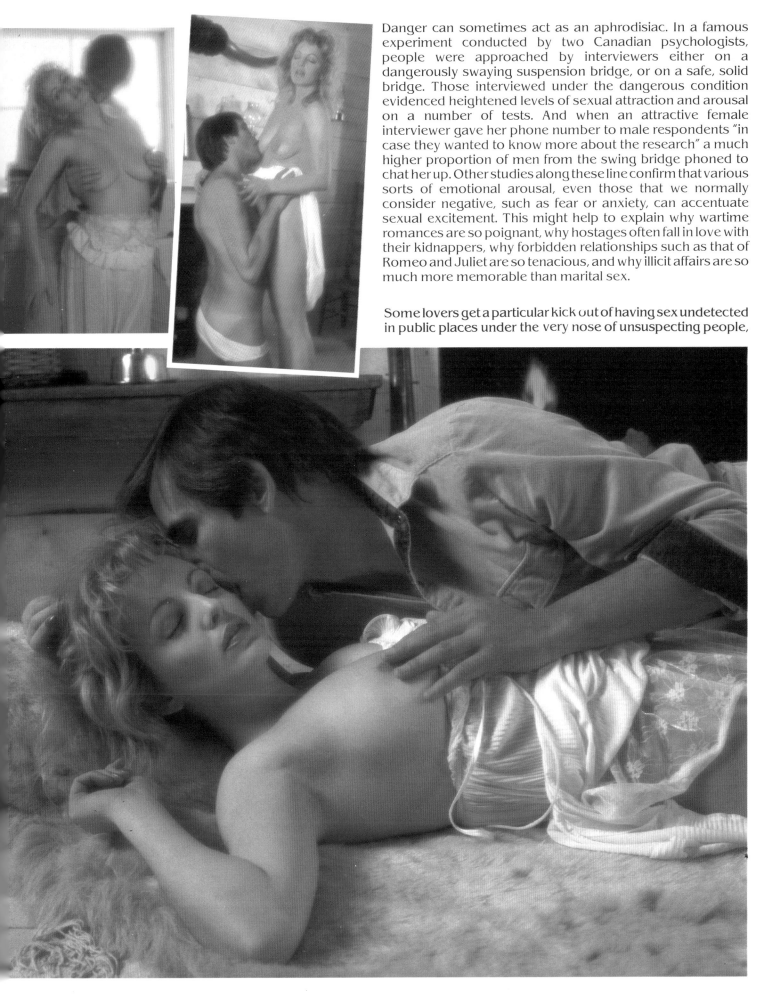

Danger can sometimes act as an aphrodisiac. In a famous experiment conducted by two Canadian psychologists, people were approached by interviewers either on a dangerously swaying suspension bridge, or on a safe, solid bridge. Those interviewed under the dangerous condition evidenced heightened levels of sexual attraction and arousal on a number of tests. And when an attractive female interviewer gave her phone number to male respondents "in case they wanted to know more about the research" a much higher proportion of men from the swing bridge phoned to chat her up. Other studies along these line confirm that various sorts of emotional arousal, even those that we normally consider negative, such as fear or anxiety, can accentuate sexual excitement. This might help to explain why wartime romances are so poignant, why hostages often fall in love with their kidnappers, why forbidden relationships such as that of Romeo and Juliet are so tenacious, and why illicit affairs are so much more memorable than marital sex.

Some lovers get a particular kick out of having sex undetected in public places under the very nose of unsuspecting people, for example while sitting on a park bench or dancing at a party. This is facilitated if the couple go out wearing no pants, or possibly no clothes at all under an overcoat. The element of 'raising the finger' to respectable society is a source of extra excitement. One young correspondent to a magazine claims to have made love to his girlfriend on several occasions while sitting on the couch watching TV with her parents. He does not seem to consider the possibility that her parents are secret voyeurs.

Night and day

Many people believe that making love at night when it is dark is the decent, natural thing to do. Nothing could be further from the truth. In the animal world, sex normally occurs in the

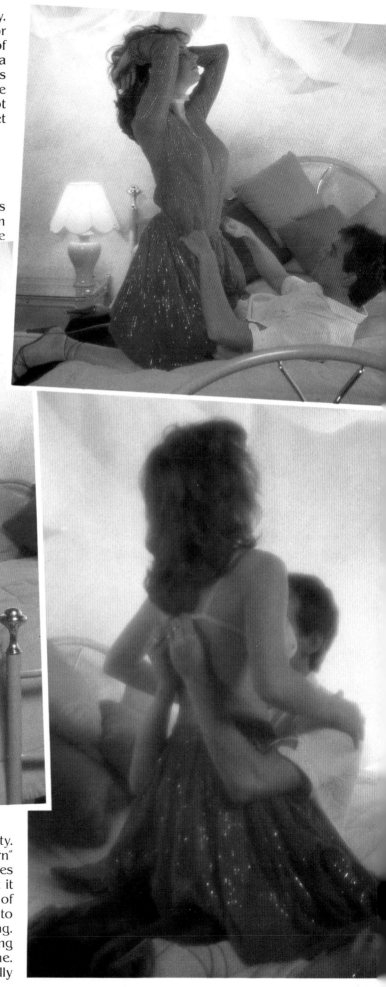

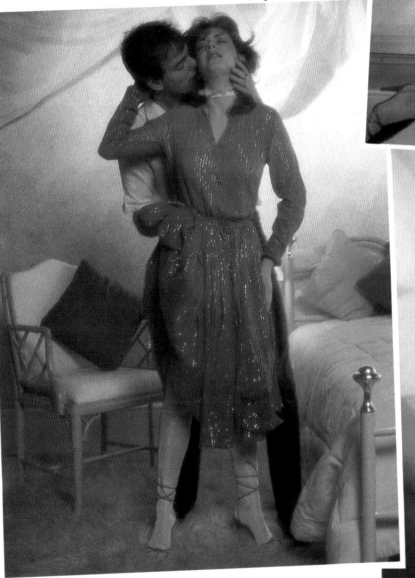

daytime, along with eating and most other kinds of activity. The night is reversed mainly for sleeping. This "diurnal pattern" is seen in nearly all mammals, including our nearest relatives among the primates, and there is reason to believe that it applies to humans also. For example, secretion of testosterone, the hormones responsible for sex drive, rises to a peak in the morning, and falls sharply in the evening. Therefore, it seems probable that our natural love-making urges are stronger when we are fresh and active in the daytime. The human shift to nocturnal sex must then be a culturally determined tendency – society prefers that we concentrate on work during the day. True, there is an instinct in animals which motivates them to seek privacy for copulation, but the cover of darkness is not a favoured solution.

Perhaps a compromise between biological and social demands is optimal. There is something particularly romantic about the half-light that is obtained at sunrise and sunset. Skin tones are enhanced by the rosy glow and blemishes are obscured. The pupils of our eyes are dilated because of the low illumination, but this may be perceived as a signal of sexual arousal. Since sexual excitement also leads to pupil dilation, a beneficient exchange is established and the couple are soon feeling very sexy. Early evening may be best of all because the day's work has been done and there is time to relax, eat, and share a drink before intimacy commences.

Sex on the move

The airline slogan "Fly United" has been satirized graphically as a pair of ducks winging along in situ. This no doubt reflects the popular belief that sex on moving vehicles is a particularly gratifying recreation. Whether it is because of the variable G forces, the regular bumps and vibrations, or the feeling of leaving past commitments behind (being "on the run") is not clear – probably all these factors are involved. The symbolic element of forsaking the past is exemplified in Erica Jong's "Fear of Flying", in which the heroine, having just left her husband and set out for Europe, has sex over the Atlantic in the aeroplane toilet to herald a new life of freedom.

People who succeed in making love in the extremely confined conditions of an aeroplane are said to become members of "the mile high club". The Victorian equivalent was sex in a railway carriage, which was a great deal more fun in the days of the luxurious, well-upholstered, separate compartments. So erotic was this setting deemed to be that leading brothels in France and Austria were equipped with special rooms done out like railway carriages, which could be mechanically vibrated and were supplied with chugging and whistling sound effects. Modern trains with their open compartments are much less attractive as sexual venues, but there is plenty of action on overnight "sleepers".

Other favourite mobile venues for sex include cars, taxis, horses, swings, motor cycles and rocking chairs. Young girls often experience their first orgasm riding solo on a horse or plummeting downwards on a swing, and the sensations involved can be even better with a partner on board. The new generation of loop-the-loop roller coasters may be tempting to some intrepid pioneers, but this could only be described as Kamikaze sex, and the reader would be well advised to keep his safety belt firmly buckled, let alone his trousers. Motor cycles may seem more virile than horses, and the leather riding gear may be a fetishistic turn-on, but don't forget they can't steer themselves if you get carried away in sexual ecstacy. Fellatio on the motorway is also a dangerous sport which is not to be recommended on grounds of public safety.

Survey findings

Scientific surveys of sexual geography are few, but several thousand readers of a newspaper recently completed a check list of the places in which they had tried making love. This study revealed a considerable amount of conservatism as well as some versatility and ingenuity. Nearly everybody had experienced sex in the bedroom and the living room, and sizeable majorities had tried the car, the bathroom, the bath itself, woods and fields and hotels. Next in order of popularity were the kitchen, private rooms at parties, public parks, beaches and private gardens. About a quarter of men responding to the questionnaire also claimed experience in water, at the office, on public transport and ships, in cinemas and theatres, in brothels, and with other people watching. The women appeared noticeably less adventurous in all of these respects. A very small proportion of men and even fewer women cited experience on motor cycles, aeroplanes, swings and lifts. Apart from any mechanical difficulties that might be encountered on such devices, some people might be deterred by the possibility of motion sickness.

When people were asked in which of these venues they had most *enjoyed* their love-making, a slightly different pattern of results was obtained. The bedroom remained the most popular choice, though much less so for men than for women. Of women, 80% nominated the bedroom compared with only 52% of men. Other locations that were favourites among the women included the living room (or lounge), woods and fields and the car and the bath. These places were all more frequently chosen by women than men. The kitchen, however, was enjoyed more by men (11%) than women (4%). Presumably women see this part of the house as symbolic of domestic subservience; or else they find lineoleum a cold and unpleasant surface to lie on. Two other minority male preferences that were not picked out at all by women were brothels and "with others watching". It seems then, that both men and women are adventurous to a degree, but men are more inclined to be kinky, and women romantic.

Some locations that were mentioned once only in the survey as places where sex was most enjoyed were: mud, a cathedral, an alley, a toilet, a window ledge, staircase, ghost train, station, barn, stable, and army barracks. Of the respondents, 5% claimed that sex was so intensely enjoyable that they were oblivious to the surroundings and regarded them as irrelevant.

One other interesting finding from this survey was a connection between people's attractiveness and their experience of sex in exotic places. People who thought of themselves as "plain" were just as likely as attractive people to have had sex in conventional places such as the bedroom and lounge, but people regarding themselves as attractive were more experienced in the romantic, outdoor places such as beaches, fields and forests, and on moving vehicles. Apparently it is the "beautiful people" who are seized by irresistible impulses to make love on the spot, whether they be swimming in the breakers at the time or riding on a motor cycle. Relatively plain people prefer to wait until they are safely tucked up in bed with the lights out before getting round to conventionally prescribed congress. The reader will no doubt now be asking himself to which group he belongs.

SOCIABLE SEX

We are all intrigued by tales of Bacchanalian orgies in the days

of ancient Greece and Rome and similar rituals attributed to primitive cultures. Men, in particular, are inclined to ponder their probable performance in such circumstances, but many women also fantasize about being shanghaied by hordes of lusty, uninhibited barbarians. Group sex themes pervade erotic literature and films, from *The Saga of Eskimo Nell* to *The Devil in Miss Jones*. Even in Gilbert & Sullivan's *Pirates of Penzance*, when a bunch of unruly pirates spring from the rocks to startle a group of Victorian maidens paddling barefoot on the beach, singing "Here's a first rate opportunity to get married with impunity", we have little doubt what they really mean.

In modern Western society, group sex has a rather different flavour. There is not so much of the unbridled lust, and even less of the rape connotation. Among the hot-tubs and redwoods of California, there grew up in the 1960s a subculture that promoted sexual pleasure as an antidote to anxiety and aggression. Underground "wife-swappers" of previous decades were soon absorbed by this "make love not war" ideology, and with the simultaneous advent of sexual equality, re-labeled themselves "swingers". This movement, albeit a minority one, soon spread to the rest of America and the capitals of Western Europe. Group sex was now morally justified as a positive, social-bonding force - a means of overcoming childish jealousies and possessiveness, and the tensions that lead to violence.

Apart from the ideological arguments, group sex has personal appeal. For one thing, it offers visual and other sensory stimulation that raises excitement to record levels, and provides fantasy fodder for some time afterwards. Some men jaded to impotence and women bored to indifference by conventional one-to-one sex may be revitalised by the group experience. Others, however, look forward eagerly to the event, but rediscover inhibitions they thought they had shaken off years ago, and fail dismally upon the day. Nobody can be sure till they've tried.

Another possible benefit of group sex is the learning experience that it provides. No longer is it necessary to base improvement of performance upon trial and error, sex manuals, or recommendations from your friends. Important tips and techniques can be gleaned from direct observation of others. Of course, for this purpose it is not necessary to trade your partner in for anyone else's; you can watch them with their own partner, then apply it with yours. Indeed, such mutual voyeurism is the preferred form of group sex for some couples.

Finally, the proponents of swinging maintain that it is the only viable way of reconciling the need for stable companionship and trust within a two-person relationship; with the generally conflicting need many people have for sexual novelty and exploration. Provided the initial shock of seeing one's partner *in flagrante* with someone else can be overcome, and the inevitable feelings of jealousy dealt with constructively in some way, then it really is possible to "have your cake and eat it". Most people control their jealousy in this situation by rational means, telling themselves that their partner is only "playing", and not investing themselves emotionally in any way; others manage to incorporate social elements such as jealousy and competition into their sexual arousal in such a way as to enhance sensation to the point of ecstacy. However,

the risk of hurt and disruption is ever present. There are bound to be "bad trips" as well as good ones, and not everybody is so sensation-seeking as to want to try in the first place.

How common is group sex? Surveys conducted in the 1960s and 70s suggested that no more than two or three percent of the population were actually involved, although a rather larger proportion (of men especially) confessed that they would like to if the opportunity arose.

EROTIC FANTASIES

More sex takes place in our minds than ever in our bedrooms. Fantasies are not the preserve of the perverted few, nor are they necessarily symptomatic of marital problems. Nearly all normal men and women have sexual fantasies at least now and again – even when their sex life is going well. It does, however, remain a very private area. Most of us would more willingly talk to strangers or fill in anonymous questionnaires than reveal our inner thoughts and fancies directly to friends, lovers or marriage partners. This is a pity, because our sex lives can often be enhanced by openly declaring them and incorporating them into love play.

We have come a long way from the dark ages of sexual repression. Many early writers of sexual fantasies, such as The Marquis de Sade (from whom the term "sadist" originates) or the Italian Pallavicino (who wrote *The Whore's Rhetorick*), were jailed or executed for their "unwholesome" contributions. Others, like "Walter", the Victorian English aristocrat who poured out his heart in *My Secret Life*, were discreet enough to remain anonymous.

Mediaeval church celibates recognized the threat to chastity posed by sexual reveries – which they called *delectatio morosa*. Penances were meted out on a scale of 25 days for a deacon, 30 days for a monk, 40 days for a priest and 50 days for a bishop. If we are to believe the impression given by Chaucer and Boccaccio of the sex lives of the clergy, it is just as well this offence is difficult to police – the likelihood of a new offence occurring before the sentence for the previous one was completed must have been considerable.

Why do fantasies occur?

The capacity for imagination is a distinctive marker of our species. Children play fantasy games from an early age, talking to imaginary playmates and transforming mundane articles into exciting beasts and machines. Indulgence in fantasy is therefore instinctual – a mental equivalent of the physical exploration that is so apparent and endearing in kittens and young monkeys. We retain this tendency in adulthood; only our preoccupations change along with the content of our mental games.

Sexual fantasies come in many shapes and forms - fleeting daydreams, extended nocturnal episodes that may culminate in orgasm (wet dreams); static visual images or ritual sequences. Sometimes they are memories of previous erotic episodes that we call up to assist with present arousal. Sometimes they are hopes concerning what ideally might happen in the future. Sometimes they relate to sexual activities that excite us as mental notions but which we know would be unpleasant or unacceptable in reality. Generally, they function to clarify our aspirations and to increase our excitement and enjoyment.

It has been said that "sex equals friction plus fantasy" and indeed, both physical and mental factors are necessary for arousal. Thus it is particularly when the social and environmental component of sex is deficient that fantasies are called upon. In masturbation, for example, the physical component is self-provided, and so must be the mental stimulation. Few people masturbate without having fantasies at the same time.

The same applies if the partner we find ourselves with is less than optimally exciting, as is the case more often than people like to admit, and may be one of the reasons for our reluctance to reveal fantasies to a partner. Some people can only successfully complete intercourse with the aid of their special fantasy. A married homosexual may be able to make love to his wife only by imagining her to be a man, and the fetishist may need to shut his eyes and think of rubber. This is why clinical psychologists are so interested in sexual fantasies; apart from their entertainment value they often provide a better clue to a person's true sexual motivation than real-life activities.

In The Whore's Rhetorick, Mother Creswel, the experienced bawd, advises a protégé as follows:

"When you are detained in ugly, sordid, or ungrateful embraces, it would be difficult without the artificial aid of a picture to counterfeit those ecstasies which every comer may expect for his money. Therefore on these occasions you must frame in your mind the Idea of some comely Youth who pleases you best, whose shadow will create a greater lust than could be raised by a nauseous though real enjoyment. The picture of this charming boy may very fitly be placed near your bed, to imprint the fancy deeper in your imagination and enable you to fall into those sweet transports which do singularly gratifie the enjoyer's heart". (English adaption, 1683).

We humans are such cerebral animals that what is going on inside our heads is often more crucial to arousal than the mere mechanics of fleshly contact. Moreover, the physical stimuli that excite us are fairly standard, whereas people vary enormously with respect to their mental turn-ons. Fantasies are idiosyncratic and tailor-made to individual requirements. The internal images formulated out of memories, aspirations, and primitive lusts too antisocial to air in reality, are pooled and refined over time so as to sharpen their excitement potential.

Fantasy partners are idealized. Air-brushed by our minds, they do not have spots or headaches. They never say "no" to our desires; they are sex-mad, crazily in love with us, and eager to fulfil all our kinky little requirements. Settings are likewise perfect. We are transported in a second to a Turkish seraglio, or to a fabulous chateau in the South of France. Overcast skies and mean streets give way to golden sunlight and palm-fringed beaches.

Fantasies may, therefore, be substitutive or compensatory, partially fulfilling frustrated wishes and improving upon non-perfect reality. Or, they may help us to plan for reality, setting up blueprints for desired targets, and rehearsing us for events that we hope to engineer, or that we fear might befall us at some stage (as in the case of rape fantasies). In all of these functions fantasies are natural, instinctual and adaptive - not pathological or perverted. They are a product of our humanity - not our bestiality.

What are the main types of fantasy?

Research using anonymous questionnaires had identified four main groups of fantasies that cluster together in the sense that the person engaging in one is likely to have the others also. These are: (1) **Intimate** fantasies, such as making love out of doors in romantic settings, having intercourse with a loved partner or someone that you know, being masturbated by a partner, kissing passionately, and having oral sex. (2) **Exploratory** fantasies, such as orgies, mate-swapping, promiscuity, being seduced as an "innocent", homosexuality and sex with someone of a different race. (3) **Impersonal** fantasies, such as intercourse with a stranger, watching others have sex, looking at pornographic pictures or films, using objects for stimulation, like dildos or candles, being excited by rubber or leather, and cross-dressing. (4) **Sadomasochism**, e.g. whipping or spanking someone, being tied up, exposing oneself provocatively, being forced to do something, and teasing a partner to distraction.

Overall, intimate fantasies are most common in both men and women, accounting for about half of all reported fantasies. They are most typical of people who have a steady partner with whom they are satisfied and in love. Exploratory fantasies are the second most common kind, but they are very much more popular with men than women. This type of fantasy is associated with a high level of libido, or need for an exciting and varied sex life. Impersonal fantasies indicate a focus on fetishes, films, clothes, and other indirect representations of sex with relatively little interest in the personality and feelings

of the partner. This tendency is also found more in men than women, and perhaps not surprisingly, is most characteristic of socially isolated men without partners. Sadomasochistic fantasies are altogether quite rare and do not necessarily imply a need to give or receive real pain in order to obtain sexual excitement. Most people whose prime fantasies are in this category are content to keep the administration of pain within the realm of fantasy. Some play harmless little games of bondage, slavery and spanking for purposes of titillation in the bedroom, but those who become rippers and rapists represent a minute proportion of men with sadistic fantasies.

It may seem surprising that sadistic and masochistic fantasies go together in the sense that the person with sadistic fantasies is also likely to have masochistic ones. This is contrary to popular wisdom that says the two are polar opposites and, therefore, should not go together. In fact, it seems that people who are interested in these areas are concerned with the connection between sex and power relationships in general. For them, the real turn-on in sex is the control that one partner exercises over the other – hence the rituals of punishment and restriction, and the role-playing scenarios of teacher/pupil doctor/patient, mother/child and so on. Since men are by nature more caught up in the struggle for social ascendancy, they are also more often preoccupied by these fringe aspects of sex. To the non-involved person it may all seem immature, but then most forms of "fun" are childish, almost by definition.

The widespread belief that the average woman is naturally somewhat masochistic and the average man a little sadistic contains an element of truth. Although woman have fewer fantasies than men that are either directly sadistic or masochistic, their fantasies do tend to be more passive than those of men. If various themes are expressed in both active (doing) and passive (being done to) form, for example "giving oral sex" and "receiving oral sex", "seducing an innocent" and "being seduced as an innocent", then men admit more to the active forms while women claim the passive ones. Insofar as fantasies bear on our real, inner nature, it does appear that women are inclined to be receptive and submissive while men are relatively active and assertive. But note, men also like to have things done to them – about as much as they like taking the initiative.

Favourite themes of men and women

Another way of finding out about people's fantasies is to ask them to write out their favourite sexual fantasy in narrative form. This has been done for large samples of people in Britain and the stories have been analysed to reveal the most popular themes. By far the most common element in men's fantasies was *group sex* or sex with two other women, "being tied to a bed with six or more naked women kissing, licking and fellating me". Nearly one third of men included elements of group sex in their prime fantasy compared with 15% of women. Those women who did favour group sex fantasies often included their steady partner or an element of force, e.g. "gang-banged by Hells Angels", "raped by the seven dwarfs".

The second most common theme in men's fantasies could be described as visual or *voyeuristic*. This usually involved reference to clothing, such as black stockings and suspenders, sexy underwear, leather, or nurses uniforms. e.g.

"A 16 year-old virgin dressed in a short-skirted school uniform and who wears a hair-band all the time". Of men, 18% included fetishistic elements like this, but hardly any women did. Other typically male elements, perhaps related to the visual emphasis, were details of anatomy, reference to the age and race of the partner, and descriptions of the sexual activity that was engaged in. Only occasionally would women refer to physical characteristics (e.g. a large penis or a black partner).

Also characteristically male were sadistic and competitive elements e.g. "Having sex with the boss's daughter on her desk with her boy friend watching but unable to do anything about it". "Me being a headmaster and my wife being a schoolgirl, and teaching her a lesson for playing with herself".

The most common element in women's fantasies was inclusion of the husband or current *loved partner* (21%). Quite a few men (14%) also featured their wife or current partner; most complimentary was the man who said "sex with two of my wife" (an interesting combination of the partner-oriented and group themes).

The second characteristically female element was reference to *exotic, romantic settings* such as islands, beaches, waterfalls, new-mown hay, space and heaven (15%) e.g. "My man making love to me on a quiet beach in the moonlight with the waves lapping over us". The partner was usually present in these settings. Many women mentioned freedom from distraction (e.g. from children or telephones) as an important aspect of their enjoyment. Only 4% of male fantasies included romantic settings such as this.

Another fairly common female element was that of *rape or force* (13%), although very often this meant being raped by the husband, partner or somebody already desired; e.g. "raped by somebody I love". A smaller proportion of men (4%) said they would like to be raped by girls, and a few fantasized total submission to a female partner.

Apparently in contrast to the idea of being roughly treated was another female fantasy of being the recipient of *chivalrous attention* and receiving gifts (4%); e.g. "Being wined and dined and romanced and then made love to on a rug in front of a coal fire". A roughly similar proportion of men fantasized female interest in them and their bodies.

Finally, 11% of women claimed to have no fantasies at all (e.g. "I don't need fantasies because I am perfectly happy with my man and my sex life"). Of men, 5% said they had no particular fantasies and 3% said they fantasized "everything".

One of the original and egocentric male fantasies was "being the women I am having sex with", and perhaps the most optimistic was "having women want me after seeing me in the centrefold of Playgirl".

Do fantasies signify frustration?

It is often thought that people have fantasies when they are not having sexual encounters. This seems to be true only for men, and then only in the short-term. Men who have been deprived of sex for a very long time, as in the case of prisoners or hospital patients, actually show a reduction in fantasy relative

Although some men may well be aroused just by the sight of a woman, particularly one undressed or undressing, most women require a longer term build up before arousal is achieved. Hence the term 'foreplay' which, as its name implies, should consist of gentle caressing, kissing and intimate fondling by both partners before actual lovemaking takes place.

to sexually active men. This is especially true of men who have little female stimulation in their environment and who have effectively given up hope of sexual conquests. For such men a kind of depression sets in which is probably related to a declining production of the male hormone testosterone.

Most women find it relatively easy to go without sex for long periods of time, and there is no reason to believe that nuns and spinsters are constantly tormented by sexual fantasies. Women, in fact, have most fantasies when they are in love and sexually active – their libido seems to be awakened by Mr Right. Far from being associated with deprivation and desperation, fantasies occur most in women who are extrovert, independent, highly-sexed and generally creative. High-fantasy women are more likely to have extramarital sex, but not because their marriages are unhappy – both seem to be reflections of a taste for life and exploration. In other words, fantasies represent a lusty libido rather than a lack of outlets.

How can fantasies be harnessed?

Fantasies may give guidance as to what we should try in real life. For instance, a girl who dreams constantly of making love to two men at the same time might consider setting it up in reality some time – it would probably not be difficult to find some willing studs. The man who frequently fantasizes about homosexual encounters might also sample the actual experience eventually.

Translating such fantasies into reality may have one of two effects: it may lead to a redirection of lifestyle and a new source of sexual enjoyment, or equally likely, it may cure the fantasiser of an obsession. Often the reality is such a let down that the fantasy is destroyed forever. This is something to consider – many fantasies are only exciting so long as they remain fantasies. They are simply not workable in reality. Of course, some violent and sadomasochistic fantasies must be kept in the domain of fantasy because they would be unacceptable to society, if not to the individual, in reality.

The other possible way of employing fantasies is sharing them with a partner so as to enhance love-making. Discussing each other's sexual fantasies is the ultimate form of communication between partners; it signifies great trust and presupposes a basically secure relationship. If couples are mature enough to appreciate fantasies as revealing mental vivacity rather than discontent, then the way is open to using them positively. This may mean dressing up and playing a role for the partner occasionally, reading them stories or whispering relevant provocative comments to them during sex. For the more adventurous, it may mean buying sex apparatus ("toys") or even including another person, who in effect becomes a living toy for the couple. (It is not impossible to find fun-loving people who enjoy being "used" in this way). Whatever the choice of adaptation, the honest revelation and sharing of sexual fantasies can add spice to an already happy relationship and may even revitalize one that is flagging.

ENHANCEMENTS

Some people are heard to boast that they like sex "plain and simple, straight up and down", and with "no kinks at all". That is all very well for people who are themselves plain, simple and straight up and down. Doubtless they prefer food unspiced and are mundane and conventional in most aspects of their lives, Other people, whom we might regard as more discerning, have a sexual appetite that is concerned not just to "fill the hole as quickly as possible", but which is, in Alex Comfort's term, "gourmet" style. These connoisseurs are aware that the pleasures of Venus are to be savoured, not devoured, and that subtle rituals, diversions, and elaborations seemingly peripheral to the sex act itself, can add sauce and spice to the consummation. In a theatrical analogy, it is clear that factors such as scenery, costumes, props, special effects and timing add a great deal of excitement to the interaction between players, and so it is with sex.

Erotica

Research suggests that the most popular bedroom titillation is looking at sexy books, magazines and pictures. More than one-third of both men and women report doing this, though precisely what kind of reading material they are referring to is not specified. To some, the lurid stories of rapist's exploits, vicar's misdemeanours and busty pin-up pictures in the newspapers may be sexually arousing, or the fairly explicit bedroom scenes to be found in most modern best-selling novels. Other people keep a private collection of more specialized pornographic material (hard-core Scandinavian magazines or classic erotica such as "My Secret Life" or "The Story of O") at hand for browsing through before love-making. Basically, erotica is a means of dealing with the need many people have for novelty and variety without threat to the primary relationship.

For a long time it has been thought that men are more aroused by pornography than women, especially pornography of the visual kind. Indeed, there is some truth to this belief which stems from the differing biological natures of men and women. However, recent research has indicated that the lack of interest in pornography previously shown by women was partly an artifact of the inadequacy of the material available at the time, which was nearly all crude, static nudity, genital close-ups and posed insertions. It is now known that while men can often be aroused by the mere sight of a nude female or a purely anatomical representation of coitus, this is seldom sufficient to excite a women. Films which show an active sequence of explicit love-making, replete with sound effects and vocal interaction, and in which the female partner is fully participant and enjoying herself, are arousing to a great many women. Movies which have some semblance of a developing plot, in which the characters are introduced and their relationships explored to some extent before action commences, are generally found to be more arousing to women than those that go straight in at the deep end, so to speak.

It has been said of the sexuality of men and women that "the engines are much the same, but the starter motors are different". Most women have a relatively cold-start, so a certain amount of patience and subtlety may be required during the warm-up phase. The new generation of unisex, soft-core erotic films such as the *Emmanuelle* series, starring Sylvia Kristel, appeal more to women than vulgar "meat market" sequences, and many an inhibited or jaded couple has benefitted in recent years from a joint visit to the cinema.

Clothing can be a powerful erotic stimulant, so don't simply rush at lovemaking; savour it, removing clothing slowly and gently. Unsatisfactory lovemaking is often due to nothing more than trying to take everything too quickly, not allowing enough time for your partner to be ready for you.

The advent of home video has made a big difference to the production of erotic movies. The market has been extended considerably to include more female viewers than was the case with the earlier "blue movie" era, and the result is that better all-round quality of production and performance is demanded. The specialist interests of leather, bondage, spanking, water sports, and so on, are still catered for, but do not feature so much in movies as in magazines. Needless to say, this market remains almost exclusively male.

Another change that has taken place over the last decade or so has been the increasing output of female-oriented novels which include increasingly frequent sexual episodes and escapades. For a long time it has been recognized that women enjoy reading romantic novels, and are usually better than men at writing them. With the combined forces of the new permissiveness and women's "consciousness", the sexual sequences in women's novels have become progressively more explicit and female-initiated, and there is little doubt that this kind of literature is titillating to many women. In California, numerous women may be observed sunning themselves beside the swimming pool, absorbed in *Fear of Flying* or the latest best-selling equivalent, and incubating fantasies preparatory to the evening's social activity.

If commercially available erotica is not to your taste you may prefer to undertake you own tailor-made productions. The simplest kind of personalized porn is the simultaneous feedback provided by the judicious placement of mirrors on the bedroom walls or ceiling (or relocating the action to some well-mirrored venue such as the bathroom). Polaroid cameras have recently found widespread application as erotic aids because feedback is fairly fast and there is no loss of privacy in developing and printing the pictures. Especially if you have your own darkroom, a camera with a tripod and delayed shutter may also make for a lot of fun. However, if you are making a permanent record of your most ecstatic moments you need to be sure of the character of your partner. Such pictures have been used for blackmail and introduced as evidence in court.

Clothing

Everyone knows that wrapped presents are more exciting than unwrapped ones. Half the fun of Christmas is in the anticipation and the conditioned excitement evoked by the patterns and colours of the wrapping paper, the bows and the bouquets. Much the same is true of human sexual arousal. Total nakedness is seldom the ultimate turn-on; rather, it is the provocative hint of partial cleavage, a nipple peering through semi-transparent lingerie; the element of tension induced by tightness, leather or elastic, or the deliberate, teasingly slow unveiling of hidden delights. These reactions have instinctual roots which are powerfully amplified by learned associations and symbols, and psychologists are only just beginning to accept that fetishistic tendencies are very common, in fact almost universal, in the human male particularly.

Puritans fear nudity for its supposed propensity to trigger lust, yet Adam and Eve may well have adopted the fig leaf to maintain flagging passion. Paradoxically, when the police arrest a streaker, or when anti-porn campaigners succeed in obtaining restrictive legislation, they not only protect on-lookers from temporary arousal, but they protect the very capacity for future arousability in these people. All societies select a taboo area of the body which must be covered for the sake of decency; although its location varies enormously from place to place and time to time, the availability of this erogenous zone means that the adjustment and removal of clothing in that area retains the power to excite libido. Nearly one in three people admit using clothes as a turn-on during love making.

The instinctual basis of fetishistic tendencies is seen in the fact that only certain types of objects and sensations are ever implicated as arousing. The objects of fetishistic excitement are usually articles of female clothing that have powerful gender associations, such as underwear, suspenders, or high-heeled shoes; or certain materials such as rubber, leather, fur or silk which have either sadistic or feminine connotations. It is no coincidence that they feel flesh-like or hair-like and that they have marked electrostatic properties (an important basis of the tickle response). Certain colours repeatedly emerge as favourites (black, red, pink and white, and various contrasts and combinations among them) and certain smells (e.g. musk, and spring flowers) also have widespread appeal. Our sexual associations are, therefore, not random but close to the presumed "innate releasing mechanisms" for human sexuality (paired, pink, fleshy hemispheres, like the breasts and buttocks, the black, hairy, public triangle, and the fatty acids produced in the vagina and under the arms). Men are more prone to the arousing effect of these stimuli than women because in the wild it is the male who normally has to initiate sex by becoming spontaneously aroused.

But learned associations are also important in sexual arousal. Evidence for the importance of early childhood experience is seen in the fact that babies' dummies and nappies crop up quite often as fetish objects and quite a few men enjoy being treated as "naughty boys" and disciplined by a very strict "mother" figure. It has been suggested that women's shoes are a very popular fetish object because they appear at ground level, which is salient to the crawling-age child.

Another critical age for the learning of fetishistic associations is adolescence, when there is a renewed influx of sex hormones like sap in the spring, and the highly memorable first sexual experiences are imprinted. For this reason some people continue to find sex most exciting in evocative but intrinsically uncomfortable situations such as behind the bicycle sheds, on top of a haystack, or in the back seat of a car. The sexual connotation of these environments comes not from our instinctual biology but from critical, formative experiences at impressionable ages. The way that our earliest partners are dressed and presented may likewise have permanent impact, such that school wear, pony tails, bobby-sox or nurse's uniforms can acquire sexual significance.

The distinction between fetishism and fashion has often been remarked upon. Fashionable clothing is a majority interest with minimal erotic significance, while fetishistic clothing holds a steady erotic fascination for the minority. Clothes that were fashionable in one era become fetish targets to some people in the next. Tightly-laced corsets, for example, were a mark of the sexually adventurous woman in the 19th Century, became the fashionable girdle of the early 20th Century, but are today a minority fetishistic concern. Stockings with

ile it is normally considered that
men are the ones to appreciate
tracted foreplay, men can also be
eficiaries.

Foreplay can be extended for as long as both parties wish before union actually takes place. Up to a point, the longer it continues, the more heightened is desire, but no rules can be laid down for the time considered 'normal'; this is a very personal matter that can only be decided on by individuals. The same is, of course, true for the sex act itself; for some it is all over very quickly, while others take much longer. So long as both partners achieve satisfaction, time is irrelevant.

suspenders were once a universal female style but since their replacement by tights for the majority of women they have taken on distinct erotic significance and were, until their recent, fashionable re-emergence, sold mainly by sex shops. It is also no accident that silky "French knickers" from the 1920s have made a big come back in the more sophisticated lingerie catalogues.

White gloves, such as were worn by ladies on formal occasions evoke excitement in some men. These are associated with hats, high-heeled shoes and handbags as pointing the extremities of the "mature women" *gestalt*. A women wearing nothing but these outline symbols may be a particular turn-on. There is a story of the lady who turned up at a highly respectable fancy dress party wearing nothing but black shoes and gloves, spreading her arms and legs and claiming to be the five of spades!

Rubber is a material that was widely used for clothing and water-proofing before the advent of plastic in about 1950. Again, the result is a hard-core of (mainly middle-aged) rubber enthusiasts and a market for rubber raincoats and aprons, sheeting, and tight-fitting garments that is primarily erotic in motivation. There is even a club, called the Mackintosh Society, which celebrates rubber fetishism in various ways, for example by holding outdoor barbecues and hoping for a rainy day. Some rubberites like to dress their women in rubber; others like the feel of it against their own skin. If the body is encased in rubber it quickly heats up and a distinctive aroma arises out of the interaction between the body itself and the surrounding material. This is said to be a great turn-on by some rubberites. Exactly why is something of a mystery; vasodilation, pheromones, electrostatics, imprinting on the smell of condoms, and tension between the conflicting associations of security and threat have all been suggested as contributing to the erotic excitement enjoyed by the small minority of enthusiasts.

In common with leather and PVC, rubber has the quality of being flesh-like in touch and resilience. Shiny black is the favourite colour for these materials, having associations of danger, sin, sadism and pubic hair. Not surprisingly, pink is the next favourite colour for rubberwear and plastic. If sufficiently thin, these materials cling to the body of the wearer, emphasizing its contours and imparting a "wet look". In this respect at least, clothing made from these materials has a fairly universal appeal and is currently quite fashionable. Specialized clothing for wearing in private, such as tight-fitting catsuits, with cut-away crotch and protruding nipples, may be purchased by mail-order, bought off-the-peg at sex shops, or commissioned from designers such as Atomage, who cater for the film industry as well as the private collector.

Equipment

Until quite recently, people who used mechanical devices in connection with love-making have been regarded as perverted, even sick. Today, vibrators are common bedroom toys, and they have the seal of medical approval, being recommended by sex therapists in connection with treatment for orgasm difficulties and impotence. Around one in five people use mechanical or other objects to enhance sexual experience and performance.

Dildo-shaped objects of one sort or another have been used by women to obtain gratification throughout recorded time, and are mentioned in the Bible ("Thou hast madest to thyself... images of men and did commit whoredom with them", Ezekiel Chapter 16 v.17). Among the favourite articles for vaginal insertion are bananas, cucumbers, candles, test-tubes (in school labs) and brush handles. It is easy to imagine what the Freudians would make of the Walt Disney film title "Bedknobs and Broomsticks". The uneven surface of corn-on-the-cob is favoured by some women, others swear by wine bottles because the flared shoulder permits adjustment to optimum width by varying the depth of thrust. (It is important to keep the bottle sealed, or the suction may cause an unsolicited hysterectomy).

Vibrators ostensibly manufactured for innocent purposes have for decades been adapted for sexual pleasure. For example, large vibro-massagers "for the relief of rheumatoid aches and pains" and the "weight reduction" belt-loops which are very exciting if positioned strategically between the legs. Today many people have "personal vibrators" which are undisguised sex toys, usually unmistakably phallic in shape. These come in many designs apart from straightforward penis simulations. Some have a "thumb" attachment so the anus can be simultaneously palpitated; some plunge in and out so as to emulate thrusting penis movements. A new type consists of a small vibrating box which attaches to the fingers by rubber rings and transfers its vibration to the genitals through the real flesh of the fingertips. A similar device is made to fit around the base of the penis so as to impart extra stimulation to the clitoris and a shuddering action to the shaft of the penis.

A number of small devices are made for women to wear unobtrusively under their clothes. These may be activated either by normal motion or by an electrical switch controlled by the user. "Love balls" consist of a pair of small balls linked by a length of cord which are inserted inside the vagina for long term stimulation. The "sex egg" (one brand of which is called "Angel's Delight) is a larger, egg-shaped vibrator that is battery operated and may be placed about the outer part of the vulva or at various depths inside the vagina.

The standard, phallus-shaped vibrators may be elaborated by fitting them inside a plastic cast of a penis. These are made to look as realistic as possible so that fantasy is added to feel, and they are given evocative names like "Big Boy", "Hot Stud" and "Deep Thrust". The sizes of phallus on display in sex shops would put most men to shame and often look quite intimidating, but the makers are presumably tuned to their customers' requirements.

Some dildoes are provided with a harness so that they can be strapped into position around the waist for simulated intercourse. Contrary to male fantasy, these are not so often used by lesbians as by sensation-seeking heterosexuals or men who lack the size, potency or staying-power to satisfy their partners. Some models are hung with testicles that may be filled with warm liquid. At an appropriate juncture this is squeezed through the phallus into the vagina to simulate ejaculation.

Vibrators are also designed specifically for anal stimulation. These are smaller in circumference and, because of the danger of them being swallowed by the rectum, they are often

equipped with a cross-piece like the hilt of a sword, which limits the depth of penetration. The stories told by physicians about patients with foreign bodies in their backsides are apocryphal: one man is supposed to have requested his doctor not to retrieve the vibrator in his rectum, just to change the batteries.

Among the imaginative range of machinery designed for male masturbation there are plastic vaginas, torsos, or even full-size, blow-up dolls that have vibrators planted inside them. With a little added lubrication, they provide a sucking action that eventually brings most men to orgasm. The most realistic dolls have hair on the head and pubis, sexy clothing, lips that allow fellatio and a built-in tape-recorder that emits ecstatic moans.

The development of vibrators has benefitted from scientific analysis in recent years. For example, Swedish neurologists have discovered that a speed of 60 cycles per second is optimal for most people. What is more, few women show any response at all if the speed is much outside of this range. It has also been found that the most sensitive parts of the body are those where mucous membrane meets the outer, dry part of the skin. This is why most women prefer not to insert vibrators inside themselves but focus on regions around the labia and clitoris. This preference of women for external stimulation of the vulva is something that men are often slow to learn. Their fantasy is penetration, but this is not necessarily the optimum pleasure for women.

One does not have to have problems to enjoy a vibrator. They do have medical uses, such as the treatment of vaginismus and the orgasmic initiation of unresponsive women. They may also be used as "comforters" in the absence of a partner, whether voluntary or involuntary, temporary or permanent. Some couples give each other vibrators as going-away presents to reduce the likelihood of extramarital affairs during a period of forced separation. But best of all, vibrators are an enhancement to love-making; for warming up the slower partner so as to coordinate orgasm, for reawakening a lazy male member, for finishing a job that was left uncompleted, or generally for having a lot of fun.

A male aid to potency that is sold in sex shops, though something of an overpriced gimmick, is the rubber penis ring. Placed around the base of the erect penis this maintains the erection for longer by restricting the outward flow of blood (erections are produced "hydraulically" by the blood supply). Carried to excess in tightness or duration this could be a dangerous practice, resulting in damage to the blood vessels.

A different principle is involved in the Blakoe Ring. This consists of a ring of ebonite that is clamped firmly, but not too tightly, around the base of the penis and underneath the testicles. A row of tiny, metal plates makes contact with the acid-secreting skin around the genitals, setting up a minute but steady electrical current. The inventor, anatomist Robert Blakoe, claims that, if the ring is worn continuously, the current stimulates the genital blood flow and the production of male hormones and sperm by the testicles, with consequent improvement in potency and fertility. Informal clinical trials indicate some benefits for men suffering partial impotence (weak or infrequent erection) though it is not clear how much of the effect is physiological and how much psychological.

S & M practices

Quite a high proportion of people are turned on by role-playing games, usually fantasies involving an exaggerated dominance and submission relationship. This group of enhancements is known as S-M, which may be interpreted as "sadism and masochism", or more broadly and accurately as "Slave and Master". Popular role assignments are parent/child, teacher/pupil, doctor/patient, rapist/victim, prostitute/client, nazi/prisoner and Roman/slave. Favoured techniques of discipline and punishment are bondage and restriction, humiliation and defilement, spanking and whipping. Standard equipment includes ropes, chains, stocks, manacles, whips, canes and chastity belts.

It is a misconception that these interests are indicative of a sick mind and are likely to lead to a search for progressive kicks that end in real brutality, criminal sadism or murder. The vast majority of S-M practitioners are quite harmless, normal people who play their games within carefully circumscribed limits and are never carried away to the point where they would ignore indications of true suffering in their partner. The slave is a voluntary and equal participant in the fun, not a true victim, and in fact usually obtains greater pleasure from the game than the master.

A second misconception is that S-M selectively exploits and demeans women. In fact, men are just as likely to enjoy the submissive role as women, and partners usually take turns in being the controller and the controlled. Of people who are strongly addicted to S-M activity, masochistic men are by far the most common, and this is reflected by the amount of pornography featuring a female "dominatrix" with boots and whip. Quite a few women make a career out of providing discipline to grown men (most of whom are otherwise normal family men, successful in business). In California there is a complete castle, equipped with torture chambers, where men with this predilection take weekend holidays. Britain has a club for S-M freaks, euphemistically called "Cooperative Motivation Research"; again the majority of members are masochistic males.

There are many theories about why people derive pleasure from S-M. One is that all our emotions have much in common, such that arousing one may be a means to enhancing the experience of another. The anticipation of sexual intercourse increases the flow of adrenalin, as does being tied up, hit by a cane or watching your spouse have intercourse with a stranger. Pain, anxiety or anger may be assimilated into sexual excitement in such a way as to amplify it. This helps to explain why "forbidden fruit" is so much more appetizing than that which is too freely available.

But this is not the whole story. In any instance there are likely to be many other contributory factors. Spanking, for example, may have a direct physiological effect of redistributing the blood supply away from the buttocks towards the genitals, thus promoting erection or clitoral excitement. It may also evoke childhood memories of chastisement that had sexual connotation deriving either from the punishment ritual itself (e.g. lowering panties and bending over) or the offence for which it was administered (masturbation or sexual curiosity). Similarly, being dressed in tight pants, clad in an all-enveloping mackintosh, or being made to crawl, could evoke early memories of a time when the child was secure in the domination of his mother, while at the same time experiencing elements of sexual awareness. The frequency with which infantile articles and activities crop up in the more bizarre forms of masochism leave little doubt that childhood experiences are involved in the establishment of our sexual partners.

Psychoanalyst Robert Stoller believes that all sexual excitement is powered by fragments of unconscious hostility, and that sexual acts represent a "revenge attack" for indignities suffered in early childhood. Although this theory need not be taken too literally, the similarity between copulation and fighting is impressive (children notoriously confuse them), and neurophysiologists tell us that the instincts of sex and aggression share many of the same cerebral circuits and hormonal triggers. Some female animals need to be chased or bitten on the neck in order to ovulate, and so a degree of aggression seems to be an integral part of mammalian love-making. The playful chasing, sparring, scratching and biting that human lovers engage in before and during intercourse has, therefore, evolutionary roots, the natural limits of which are hard to specify, and it is not much of an extension that rape and domination fantasies are also derivative of such instincts.

Another element in S-M motivation may be the attempt to gain control of our fears. Some mountaineers admit that they are terrified of heights and of falling, and paradoxically climb mountains in order to combat this fear. Similarly, the man who arranges for his wife to have intercourse with another man in front of his eyes is unlikely to be free of jealousy; more likely he is attempting to overcome his worst fears by facing them head on. This is a well recognized clinical technique for the treatment of phobias, called "implosion therapy". Since the situation has been deliberately arranged, the "victim" can experiment with his feelings while maintaining a measure of control over the proceedings. He may even be able to "sugar the pill" by transferring his jealous arousal to sexual excitement.

Perhaps the most important aspect of S-M to understand, is its ritual and magical significance. Ritual slows down the performance so that excitement has time to build gradually to new heights of ecstacy. Restraint, ordeal and chastisement offer expiation of guilt and expand the boundaries of awareness, much the same as in yoga and religious ceremonies. As with other forms of "magic", historic settings, hoods and robes, tests and incantations, soft lighting and music, and menacing images and devices are used to stimulate the imagination and create an atmosphere of unreality. In the use of commands, bondage, suspense and mild pain infliction, the "master" gives to the "slave" relief from responsibility, new powers and transcendent experiences, rewards that are in many ways parallel to those obtained by religious mystics. To view such mind-expansion procedures in terms of psychiatric pathology is to do them a great injustice. Human beings are naturally exploratory creatures, and this applies to their mental experiences as much as physical geography.

Aphrodisiacs

The search for substances that promote libido and virility has been as long and ardent, and almost as fruitless, as the search for the philosopher's stone. Of the many foods and spices that have been claimed as sexual rejuvenators (ginseng, garlic, ginger, vanilla, sarsparilla, liquorice, passion flower, pumpkin seeds, betelnuts, vitamin E, caviar and oysters) most are generally healthy additions to the diet but have no clearly proven specific effect upon sexual prowess.

The male sex hormone testosterone (prescribed by doctors under the name *potensan forte*) will restore sexual interest in men whose own supply is lacking for any reason (e.g. castration or old age), but they have no impact on the normal man. Male hormones will increase libido in the majority of women, but because of the danger of general masculinization (e.g. hair on the chin), doctors are more likely to recommend the topical application of testosterone directly onto the clitoris. This increases sensitivity and sexual responsiveness in a woman without the side-effects of systemic hormone alteration. Oestrogen replacement therapy may, however, be useful in maintaining sexual functioning in post-menopausal women.

Certain drugs such as mescaline, cocaine, marijuana and amyl nitrite can enhance sexual experience (just as they enhance any experience, whether it be colour, music, fear or grief). However, there are certain dangers associated with them, not least the danger of being arrested and put into jail, since they are all illegal.

The most famous aphrodisiac of all, Spanish fly, is also the most dangerous, and its use should never be contemplated. This is a drug called *cantharidin* derived from a dried insect. Taken internally, it produces irritation of the stomach, kidneys and urethra, which might temporarily be mistaken for sexual excitement, but even a few crystals are likely to be fatal. Strychnine has a similarly fine threshold between stimulant and deadly poison and should, therefore, never be experimented with.

In recent years there has been much interest in the possibility that human pheromones might be chemically synthesized and marketed as sex attractants. These are organic chemicals rather like sex hormones which are emitted by an animal in order to turn on members of the opposite sex through the sense of smell. Their effectiveness is much more obvious in non-human animals. Musk, the prime component of most perfumes, is a pheromone produced by the scent glands of a male deer in order to attract females during the rutting season. Its smell is not unlike some human sexual attractants, particularly those produced in the armpits and genitals of men, and most people do find it exciting to some extent. A pheromone called *androsterone,* found in the sweat and urine of male pigs, has for some time been marketed under the name *Boarmate* as a leg-opener for reluctant sows. Since this is also produced by the human male, and some research seemed to suggest that it attracted women, it has become available in sex shops as a spray-on aphrodisiac. Its efficacy is scientifically dubious, however, and most women say that in concentrations high enough to smell at all it smells revolting. There is also a female pheromone called *copulin* produced in the vagina, which might account for the popularity of cunnilingus, but so far no attempt has been made to exploit it commercially.

Aphrodisiacs do exist, then, though their effect is individual and somewhat elusive. The vast majority are ineffective (like rhino horn), illegal (like mescaline), dangerous (like Spanish fly), or all three of these at once. For most practical purposes we are better off sticking to the age-old, well-established aphrodisiacs - beauty, power and pornography.

MEN: HOW TO SEDUCE A WOMAN

1. Show that you are interested

Make your intention explicit but not your language. Engage her in warm, appreciative eye contact. Say "I want you" through your smiling eyes rather than with words.

2. Get her off her own territory

Arrange your meetings at your place rather than hers, or in a romantic setting that is novel to her, be it a bar, restaurant, art gallery, concert or holiday town. If activities like sailing or dancing are involved, they should be things at which you are competent.

3. Show ego-strength and security

Don't talk about yourselft excessively, especially not in a neurotic or boastful way. Don't try too hard to sell yourself – this suggests you think you're not really good enough for her and she is bound to accept your own evaluation.

4. Compliment her and provide for her

Make credible comments, not transparent flattery. Show that you are a good provider by presenting her with personal gifts such as flowers, perfume, jewellery, or clothing, and buying her good meals.

5. Organize distracting and relaxing stimuli

Soft lights, music, natural settings of trees, flowers, beaches, warmth and alcohol are all conducive.

6. Maintain control

Convey your own confidence; always assuming your success. The prime rule of military and other discipline is "never give an order that you think might be disobeyed". Likewise, the man should never make a move that he thinks might be blocked or rejected by the woman.

7. Tantalize

Don't invade her space or touch her before she is really ready and always hold something in reserve. Find an erogenous zone that is not too obvious and threatening, e.g. the neck or ear lobe, and do not progress beyond that until she is craving for you to do so.

8. Be sensitive

Remember that each woman must be treated as an individual. Learn about her and watch how she responds to your

Rear entry is every bit as natural and comfortable as the frontal positions although, of course, face-to-face communication is not possible. (Previous pages, main picture): **Capuchin**, in which his legs are positioned outside hers. (Inset, top centre) is shown **Her-Desire**, an oral sex position.

This page features **Half-Free-Spread** (above) and **Entwined** (right).

Overleaf are shown: **Revenge** (main picture), **Appeasing-Position** (inset, top left) and **Entanglement** (inset, top right).

attentions. Be ready to modify your strategy at any point, and never let your technique show.

WOMEN: HOW TO SEDUCE A MAN

1. Appear clean

Wash your hair and hands in particular, and be bathed and sweet-smelling throughout. Don't smoke, especially if he doesn't, and clean your teeth.

2. Wear provocative clothing

Not too tarty and unsubtle; not too formal like a *Vogue* model. Let it show your best attributes in an enticing, natural way. Appear touchable – not trussed up and inaccessible.

3. Act coy and coquettish

Be caught looking at him admiringly, perhaps over the shoulder of someone else you are talking to. Show embarrassment and sexual awareness by averting your gaze and blushing.

4. Don't talk too much

Maintain some mystery. Talk in low tones. Avoid discussion of intellectual topics like politics and religion, or even sex. Never mention women's rights, marriage, babies, orgasms or your husband (unless to say that he is going away).

5. Be flirtatious

Do something cheeky that invites chase or punishment. Torment or provoke him in some minor way so as to arouse his male need to dominate. If you are dancing with someone else, make a sexy display while throwing glances at him.

6. Make him feel superior

Ask him to instruct you in something that he is good at, e.g. playing pool, driving, tennis, swimming, astronomy. Sports that involve physical demonstrations are particularly advantageous.

7. Be amusing and light-hearted

Don't be heavy and serious all the time. Be playful and make him laugh – but not by telling long-winded set jokes.

8. Use symbolic caresses

Play with the salt-cellar suggestively. Caress your own lapel or thighs dreamily. Open your lips and run your tongue along them so as to moisten them tenderly. Finally, don't say "what kind of girl do you think I am?" when the guy responds to all this.

HOW TO BE LOVED

Finally, some people look to the long term and want to know how to make someone fall in love with them for all time. The answer is not to seek love too directly, for then it is the most elusive. Outright assertion that you are looking for a mate, wanting to get married, or trying to fall in love are usually counterproductive. They are egocentric and unattractive because they take no consideration of the needs of the other person and cast them in the role of "victim".

The best way to be loved is to bestow love. You have to give in order to get. People love you for the person you are and the things that you do. You cannot demand love from others; it is an attitude they must arrive at freely and spontaneously. Therefore, work on yourself, not your target. Strive to be a better, more charming, unselfish, and witty person than you are at present (and don't say that's not possible).

If you have found a mate and want them to love you more than they appear to at present, then the important thing is to take a genuine interest in them. This means to listen to them, understand them, be warm, supportive and non-possessive. Don't put them in chains and inhibit them from revealing thoughts that are unflattering to you – try to make your love as unconditional as possible.

Show that you care by doing little things for them – making coffee in the morning, arranging outings or entertainment. Buy them little things which cost hardly any money but connect in a personal way and show that you think about them. An out-of-season present (one that is not socially obligatory) counts for more than the ritual gifts of Xmas or birthday. Initiate little sexual escapades at "inappropriate" times. Don't always leave it to your partner to put you in the mood, and don't allow sex to become routine in style, location or time of day. Actually, the rules for enjoying love are the same as those for enjoying life itself. Be fun, play games, retain a sense of humour, and of childlike excitement with the world. Use your imagination to breathe life into routine situations.

To maintain love for any length of time it is necessary to beware the green-eyed monster. Jealousy should be avoided as far as possible, or at least the righteous display of it. Jealousy is natural and fairly universal, but it is seldom attractive, and often destructive. Remember that it is a selfish, childish emotion that needs to be contained, not something to be proud of. Your mate will soon cease to love you if they begin to see you as bent on curbing their freedom, adventure and pleasure in life.

Accept that few people, male or female, are cut out for a life-time of monogamous devotion and passion. Your mate is bound to be attracted to other people at times, or at the very least curious about them, but this does not mean they value you less. It helps if you can learn to "twist the tail" of jealousy, using the passion it creates constructively, for example, by encouraging your partner's exploratory instincts in fantasy and enjoying their lust vicariously.

Be prepared for your relationship to evolve from teenage mania and entrancement to adult warmth and companionship. Try to turn your lover into a friend if you wish to be with them forever. You should learn to control jealousy, but on the other hand you should not provoke jealousy in your partner unnecessarily by cruel deceit and humiliation. Consider their feelings, keep them reassured and never underestimate their intelligence, awareness or sensitivity.

Counter-Front (right) can be achieved
only when a high degree of sexual
excitement is attained, while Roll-
Position (below) involves both partners
in rolling, while entwined, so that
first one, then the other is on top.

Sleeper is the name of the position
(bottom), regarded as one of the most
comfortable.

Holding his partner's hips well off the
floor, Arm-High (facing page) is
achieved.

In **High-Thigh-Embraced** (above) both of
her legs embrace him at the hips or
thighs.

Free-Spread (right) is made more
comfortable if a cushion or pillow is
placed under her back.

(Facing page) is shown **Soled-Over**, and
(overleaf, left) the more energetic
Wheelbarrow-Dance. The reverse of this,
titled simply **Wheelbarrow**, is shown
(overleaf, right).

Requiring a degree of physical strength in both partners is **Pillar** (right).

The illustration (facing page) shows **The-Trestle**.

These oral sex positions are known as: **Subjugator** (far right), **Instinct** (below) and **Prone-Pivot** (overleaf).

Greater or lesser degrees of difficulty are exemplified by the positions shown on these pages and overleaf.

(Top left) is **Entwining-Spine**, (above) is **Sinking-Squat** and (left) is the reverse rear-entry **Balanced-Spike**.

On the facing page are shown: (top) **Duck** and (bottom) **Projection**.

The positions overleaf are named **Double-Knee** (left) and **Double-Kneel** (right).

Levrette This is an age-old method of rear entry (left) in which she kneels on all fours with her thighs spread far apart. He kneels behind her with the upper part of his body horizontal.

Wild-Push is a variation (below) on the rear entry position in which she stands with feet apart and bends over, reaching forward with hands on the floor and, on entry, she can push backwards in time with his movements.

Pegasus A very energetic variation (facing page) in which he first squats on the floor and, after entry, grips her firmly while she reaches back holding his upper arms. He then gradually rises to a standing position and she extends her legs backwards to maintain balance.

Pillar The couple stand chest to chest (below left), sexually united. His hands grip her around her back, she locks her arms around his shoulders, then raises her legs to grip him around the waist.

Illustrated on these pages are variations on oral sex positions. The positions themselves: **Arch** (facing page); **Head-Dive** (top left; **Veneration** (top centre); **Backward** (top right); **Merry-go-Round** (above) and **Wonder** (left) are self explanatory and all afford either stimulation, satisfaction or both.

Overleaf are shown two further variations in this group: **Back-to-Belly** (left) and **Squatter** (right).

Two rather more exotic, and athletic, oral sex positions: the **Horizontal** (main picture) and the aptly-named **Acute-Angle** (inset).

A restful position, the **Eagle-Act** (facing page) contrasts with the far more athletic **Plunge** (right) which requires a chair, or similar support, that is firm enough not to slip on the floor, on which he rests his arms to regulate penetration.

In the **Wheelturn** (above) he takes on a completely passive role while she, as the name of the position suggests, can turn according to the preferences of both partners.

The bedroom is not the only place where lovemaking can be enjoyed; indeed, variation of the venue can often add an extra degree of stimulation to the act. Warm – not hot or cold – water running over the body is pleasantly relaxing and this, together with the added pleasure of foreplay, as illustrated on these pages, can be highly enjoyable.

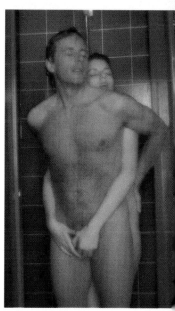

Bathing, or showering, before making love adds greatly to the enjoyment of the act, and when two people share the same shower the pleasure is heightened enormously. Each partner washing the other is an act of intimacy in itself and, with care, there is no reason at all why lovemaking should not take place here as anywhere else.

As its name implies, **Double-Kneel** (overleaf, left) is accomplished with both partners kneeling and is an ideal position for a shower cubicle, as is **Climbing-Ivy**, illustrated (overleaf, right).

ssandra (facing page) is very similar
Vault-Brace (above) except that, in
former, both partners have lowered
mselves to the floor of the shower
icle.

Care should obviously be exercised with
regard to the slippery floor of the
shower (top right) but oral sex can be
enjoyed in all its forms by either
partner (right).

A slight variation on the position known as **Vault-Brace** is shown (above) while that (top right) is known as **Three-Supports**.

The position for oral sex, known as **Veneration**, is illustrated (right) and (facing page) is the sex position **Bevel-Brace.**

The maxim to follow in foreplay is "take it slowly". Whenever possible start at the top and work downwards. Don't think of clothing as an obstacle, but rather as the packaging on something to be prized; there is enjoyment in savouring the undressing, a little at a time, and items of clothing, such as a bra, stockings and panties can be sexy toys in their own right. Moving your hand under your partner's skirt can be a powerfully erotic sensation for both of you, so linger over it, enjoying it to the full before you progress to complete lovemaking (overleaf).

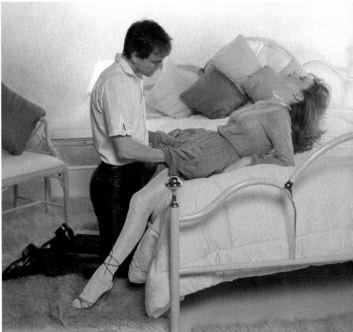

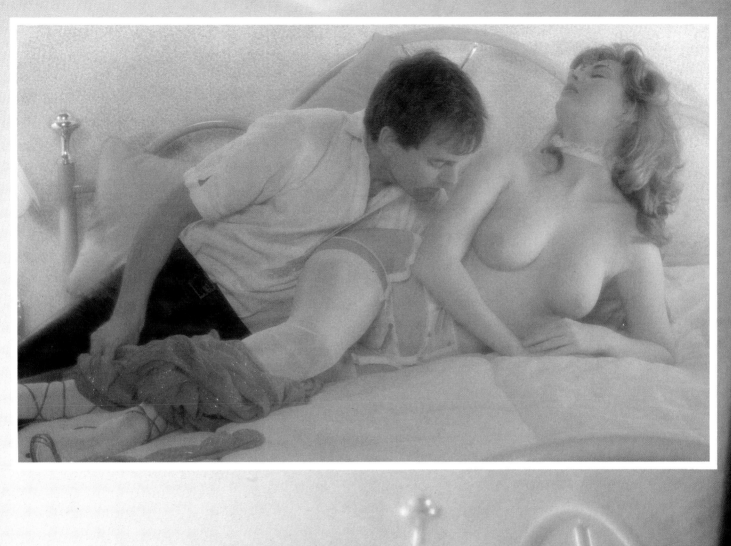
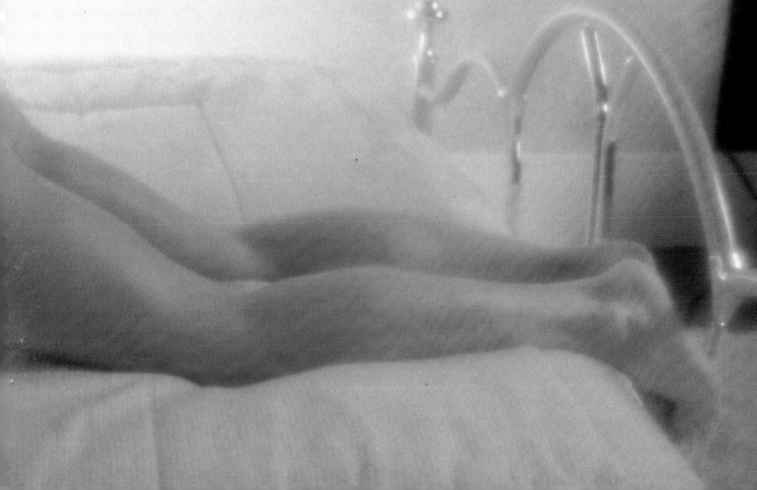

(Top left) is shown the position **Wheel-Edge** and (top right) **Arch-Thrust**, a restful position, in which she slides down the backrest formed by his thighs to achieve union. **Negresse** is seen (above) which, because of the comparative freedom of her legs, permits a great number of variations.

Peak-Squat (facing page) allows only shallow penetration, as does **Knee-Ride** (overleaf), unless she leans forward, when it can be as deep as she wishes.

The embrace (inset, right) is
known as **Thigh-to-Thigh**, in which
her legs are kept closed, with
his legs wrapped around them.

Bend-and-Sink (main picture)
may best be desribed as "reverse
rear entry" and is a position in
which variations are probably
superfluous.

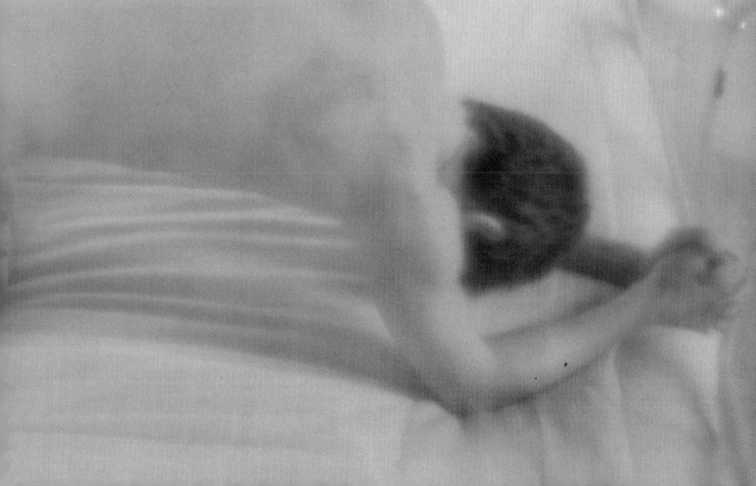

Shown on these pages are: **Mourette** (facing page); **Spine-Squat** (top left); the twisting position known as **Counter-Flank** (top right) and the rather more energetic **Impetuous** (above).

(Overleaf): the main picture shows a slight variation on the latter position, while **Border-Bias** (top left) requires some care, by both parties, in balancing.

The picture (top centre) features the rear entry position **Under-Thrust** and that (top right), with his legs outside hers, allowing minimal penetration, is called, simply, **Thrust**.

Entwined thighs give **Spring-Fork** (top left) its name and **Crouch** (top right) is equally descriptive. Deep penetration can be achieved with variations on **Press** (above) but this is not the case with **Night-Mare** pictured (facing page, top). A restful rear entry position is afforded by **Cuissade** (facing page, bottom). (Overleaf) **Span-Ride**.

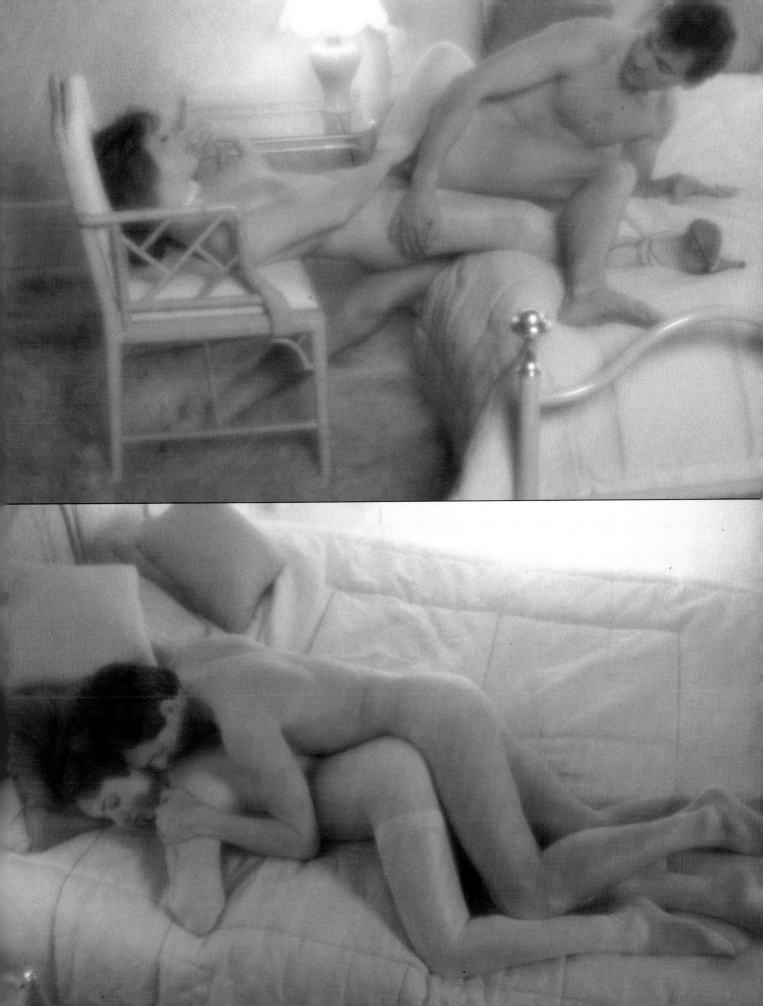

The chair and bed used on the previous page can again be utilised in attempting the rather difficult position (above) called **Sole-Prong**.

Shown (left) is a straightforward position, **Polychrest** and (right) is **Morning-Thorn**.

Two frontal and one rear entry positions are shown overleaf: **Dulkamara** (inset, top left), the well-named **Edge-Spring** (inset, top right) and **Level-Push** (main picture).

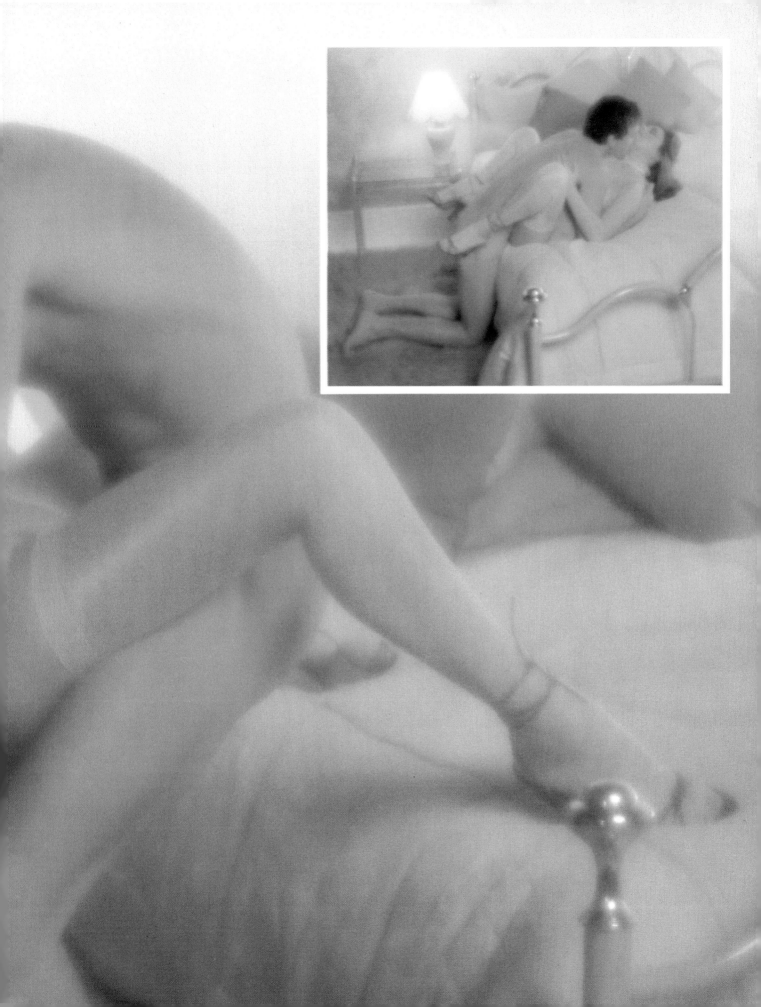

Previous pages: **Breakers** is illustrated (left) and **Wild-Prop** (right).

These pages: **Backward-Suspension** (right), **Probe** (below), **Revolt** (bottom), **Counter-Volte** (facing page, top) and **Plunge** (facing page, bottom).

Overleaf: the contortionistic position known as **Wild-Stretch-Prize**.

(Overleaf) three less demanding positions for love-making: the main picture shows **Diagonal-Dart**; (inset, top left) is **Spine-Squat** and (inset, top right) is **Wheelturn**, a position which allows several variations.

For some of the positions shown, in particular **Berserk-Flag**, (illustrated facing page), considerable physical strength is required. Also shown on these pages are: **Fall-Prop** (top); **Tigress** (left) and **Croupade** (above).

Crossed (top left) takes its name from the fact that, initially, both partners assume attitudes at an angle to each other although, by leaning forward, he can still caress her. In the position known as **Great-Flank** (above) one of her thighs is trapped between his, with her trapped leg resting on a stool or chair.

Knees-High (left) is considered a comfortable position by reason of its restful nature.

Requiring rather more dexterity and balance is **Balance-Lift** (facing page).

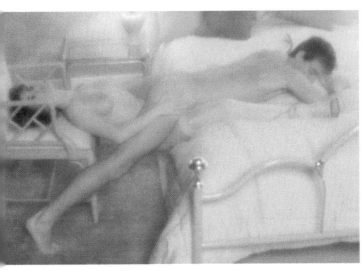

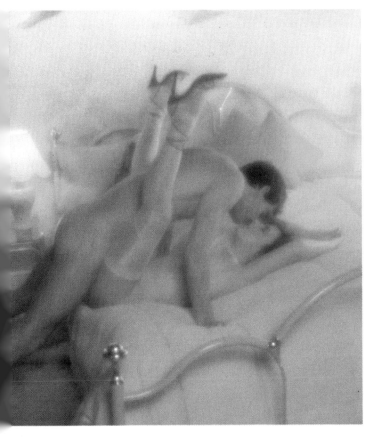

Once again, physical strength is required in successfully achieving positions such as **Climber** (facing page) and **Fata-Morgana** (overleaf left). Of the remaining positions, only **Night-Nymph** (top left) and, perhaps, **Rebel** (above centre) are at all difficult to achieve. **Makeshift** is shown (top right); what might be considered a variation of it **Wheel-Edge** (left), and **Double-Prong** (above). (Overleaf right): an oral sex position known as **Acrobatics**.

Somewhat precarious, and requiring a firm support, is **Chair-Drop** (facing page). Three positions for oral sex, **Walk-Around** (top left), **Chute** (top right) and **Pendulum** (overleaf, main picture), are illustrated. A reversal of many of the positions, in which she lies between his legs (left), is known as **Double-Prong**. Shown (above) is **Norne** and (overleaf, inset) is **Spring-Tongs**.

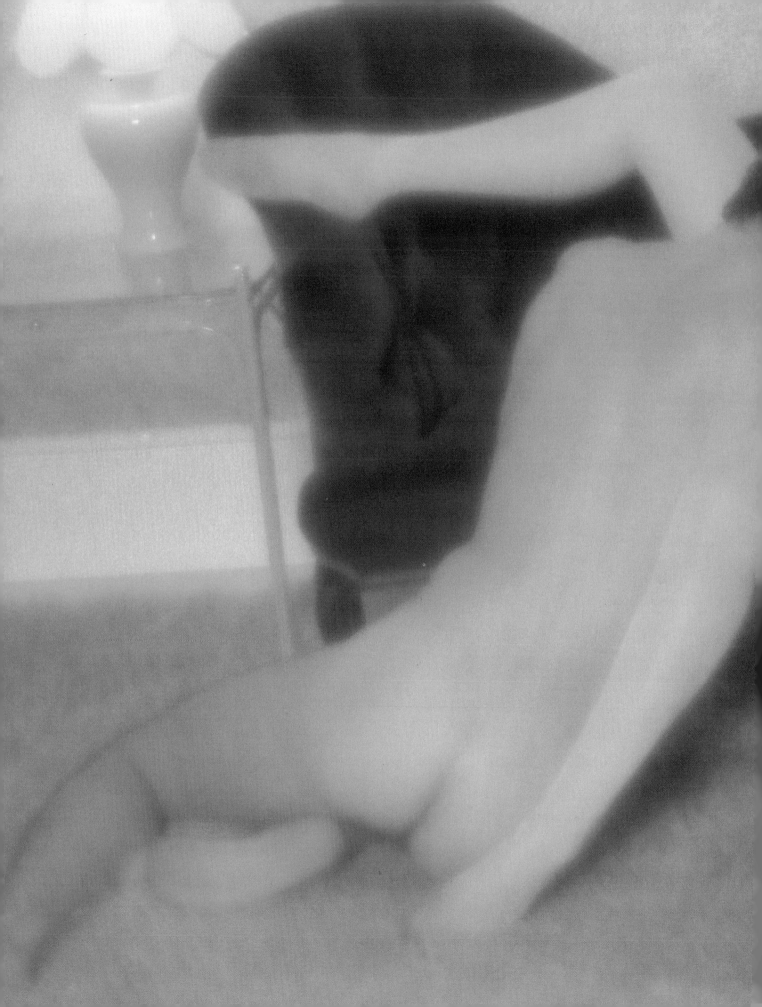

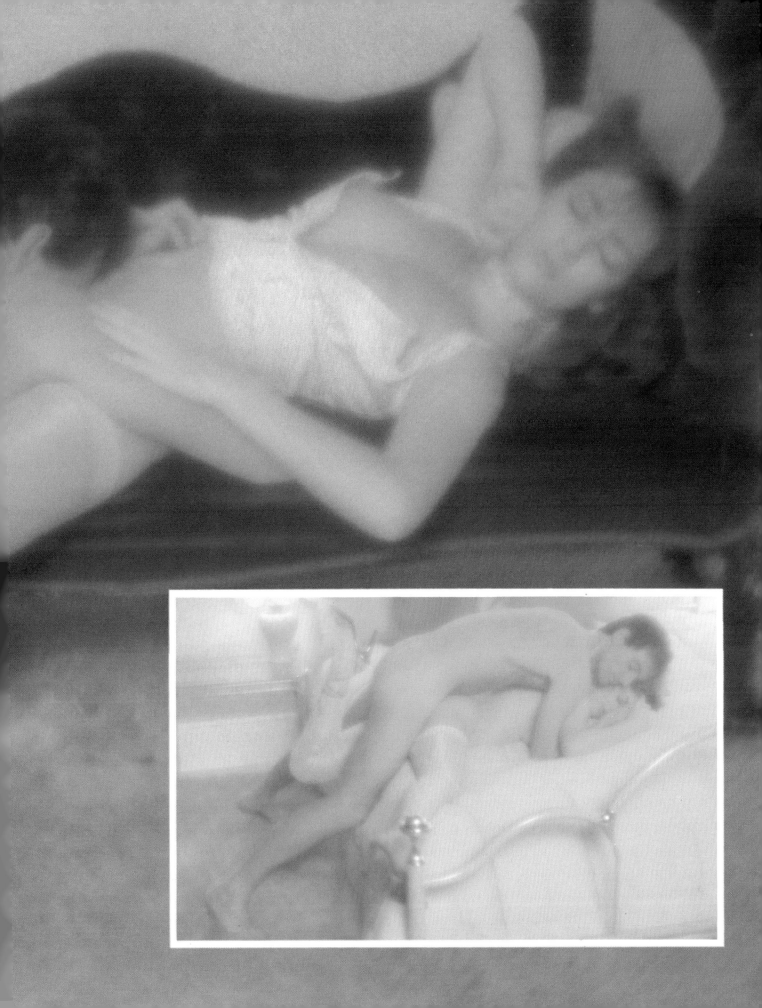

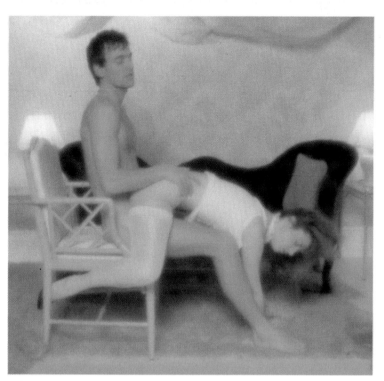

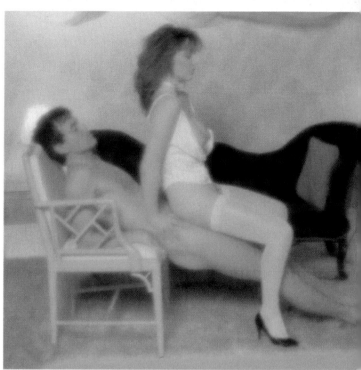

Various items of furniture, such as the chair featured here, can be utilised in achieving the positions shown: **Solar-Transit** (top left), **Express** (top right), the rather difficult variation on **Fata-Morgana** (left), the squatting position known as **Saving-Clause** (facing page), and (overleaf) **Level-Riding** (main picture), **Passion-Pranc** (inset, bottom left) and **Onward-and-Upward** (inset, bottom right).

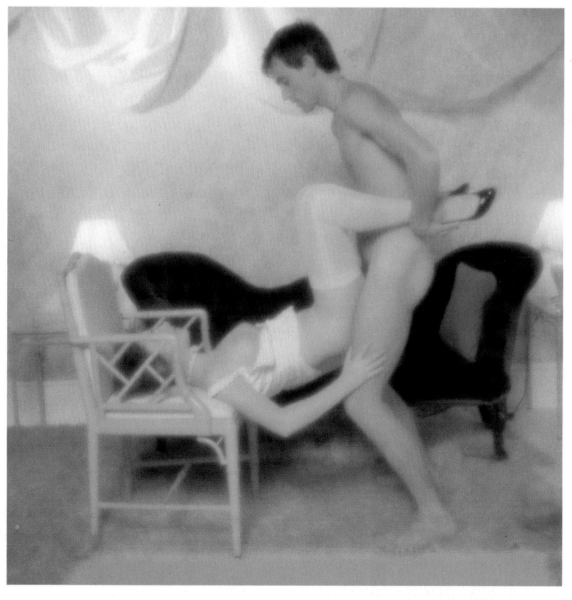

Although a rocking chair is used for these illustrations, and while it has, because of its movement, certain advantages, take care not to become too carried away in the passion of the moment, otherwise an exciting session of lovemaking could result in an upset!

(Left) is shown **Pulley-Jack**, (bottom left) **Obstinacy**, (below) **Interlink** and (facing page) **Straddlethorn-Split**.

The bench obviously supplies a more secure support for **Special-Delivery** (left) while the chair provides the right amount of rocking movement helpful in gaining the full degree of pleasure from **Novel-Cross** (top left), **Galatea** (top right), **Purification** (above) and **Plunger** (facing page).

Again utilising the bench as a firm support are the positions shown overleaf, known as: **Cavalry-Retreat** (main picture), **Bench-Privilege** (inset, top left) and **Penthesilea** (inset, bottom right).

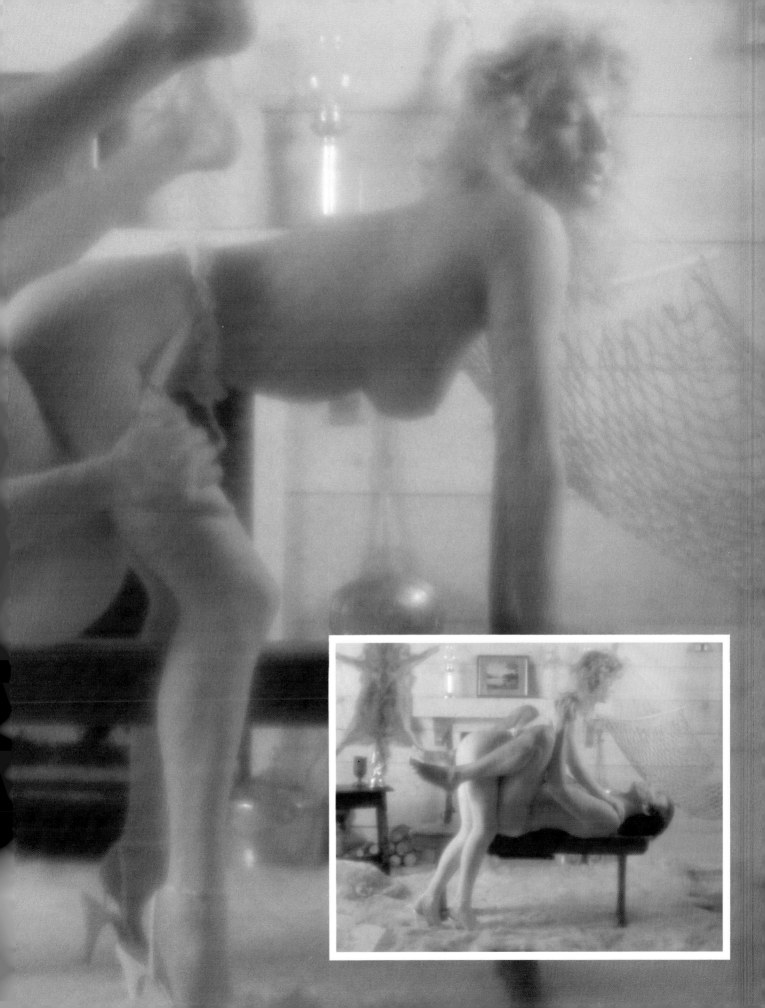

Useful motion is provided by the
rocking chair used for **Caper** (top left),
Cantilever (above right) and **Single-
Mounting** (facing page) while, in
addition, considerable strength is
needed for **Barrier-Slope** (above left)
and **Interregnum** (top right).

The same setting and chair is again utilised in showing: **Inclination** (left), **Triumphal-Arch** (below), the legs-entwined position **Flanking-Nest** (facing page), and a second chair is brought into use for **Reverse-Ride** (below left).

The hammock utilised in **Come-On-Stance** (facing page) is both ideal for the position and much safer than the rocking chair.

Shown (left) is **Hook-And-Eye**, (below left) is **Sleighride** and (below) is the position known, for reasons not obvious, as **Scotsman's-Leap**.

Considerable gymnastic ability is required should the position (overleaf) for enjoying oral sex **Horizontal** style wish to be attempted.

Serving a similar purpose to the rocking chair, but capable of more varied movements, and certainly safer, a hammock is employed in the illustration of the position called **Divebomb** (left). **Spirited** is shown (below), **Pearls** (facing page, bottom) and a variation named **Braiding** (overleaf). Those depicting oral sex are: **69** (facing page, top left), **Hunter** (facing page, top right) and **Over-The-Fence** (bottom).

Pine-covered walls, a rug, a log fire and: **Triangle** (facing page, top), **Up-Front** (facing page, bottom), **Wheeler** (left), the singularly-titled **N** (below) and, a conclusion for a night of love, **Night-Watch** (bottom).

Continuing with oral sex positions, on this page we have: **Over** (top left), **Above** (top right), **Dog-Fashion** (above) and **Baby** (right).

The sex variations on the facing page are termed: **Wild-Cross** (top) and **Steep-Squat** (bottom).